Muhammad Ari Pratomo

PROFESSIONALS UNDER THE ALGORITHM SPOTLIGHT

Ethics, Image, and Competition in the Digital Age

PROFESSIONALS UNDER THE ALGORITHM SPOTLIGHT
Ethics, Image, and Competition in the Digital Age

Muhammad Ari Pratomo

Published by PT MuhammadAriLaw Pustaka Nada, 2025.

Published By :
PT MuhammadAriLaw Pustaka Nada
Citra Indah City Housing Complex, Bukit Azalea AF 7 No. 3
Jonggol, Bogor Regency, Indonesia 16830
Website: https://www.mpnpublishing.com
E-mail:ptmuhammadarilawpustakanada@gmail.com
Tel.: +628115222152
Writer
Muhammad Ari Pratomo
Layout Designer, Front and Back Cover
Muhammad Ari Pratomo
Page: v + 147 ; 14.8 cm x 21 cm
Edition: 1, September 2025
Publisher:
PT MuhammadAriLaw Pustaka Nada
Citra Indah City Housing Complex, Bukit Azalea AF 7 No. 3 Jonggol, Bogor Regency, Indonesia 16830
Website: https://www.mpnpublishing.com
E-mail:ptmuhammadarilawpustakanada@gmail.com
Tel.: +628115222152

PROFESSIONALS UNDER THE ALGORITHM SPOTLIGHT ETHICS, IMAGE, AND COMPETITION IN THE DIGITAL AGE

First edition. September 5, 2025.

ISBN: 979-8232317836

Written by Muhammad Ari Pratomo.

Table of Contents

Foreword

In this digital age, we are witnessing profound changes affecting nearly every aspect of professional life. Lawyers, doctors, lecturers, accountants, consultants, and many other professionals no longer work solely in offices, clinics, or courtrooms. They are now also in the public spotlight, amplified by social media, algorithms, and popularity culture.

This spotlight presents two opposing sides. On the one hand, social media provides opportunities to expand reach, build image, and introduce work and services to the public. However, on the other hand, this spotlight often becomes a trap: encouraging professionals to pursue popularity over upholding the ethical code that has long been the foundation of their profession.

This book serves as both a guide and a reflection. It not only addresses the ethical challenges of navigating social media algorithms but also offers a framework and strategies for professionals to maintain integrity, build a healthy image, and survive the image battles of the digital world.

It is hoped that this book can serve as a moral and practical compass for anyone in a profession with public responsibility, preventing them from losing their identity amidst the torrent of virality. Ultimately, integrity is the primary foundation that distinguishes a true professional from a mere popular figure.

Enjoy reading, reflecting, and hopefully this book will inspire you to remain steadfast as a professional with integrity, even under the spotlight of algorithms.

Jakarta, September 3, 2025

Muhammad Ari Pratomo

CHAPTER 1

A New Era in the Spotlight

In the past, a professional's reputation was built slowly. A lawyer was valued for his experience in the courtroom, a doctor was respected for his dedication in the practice room, and a lecturer was respected for his scientific work. This process required time, consistency, and recognition from both peers and the wider community.

But now, that landscape has changed drastically. The digital age has given rise to a new spotlight that is no longer solely determined by tangible achievements, but also by algorithms a series of hidden logics that govern what appears on everyone's device screens. Social media and search engine algorithms determine who is seen, who is marginalized, and even who is trusted.

A doctor may become more well-known not because of the number of patients they cure, but because of their viral medical content. A lawyer may garner more public attention from their comments on social media than from their arguments in the courtroom. The same is true for other professions: algorithms have become the new "spotlight," elevating some to the center stage while leaving others in the shadows.

This shift raises fundamental questions: has the measure of professionalism shifted from competence and integrity to digital popularity? Can the image created by algorithms truly reflect a professional's qualities, or does it simply mask substance with a false gloss?

This new era requires every professional to understand how algorithms work, not just to compete in the spotlight, but to maintain their professional identity. Ethical awareness is crucial: how to appear in the digital space without losing one's essence, how to utilize technology without being enslaved by its logic, and how to remain trusted not just because of algorithms, but because of real quality.

In the past decade, the measure of professional success was relatively clear. A lawyer was measured by the number of cases won or their contributions to the development of law. A doctor was judged by their clinical expertise, scholarship, and dedication to patients. A lecturer or academic was valued for their scientific work, teaching, and contributions to the scientific community. All of this required a long, gradual process, and peer recognition.

However, the situation is different now. The era of algorithms has transformed the way the world sees and judges. Social media, search engines, and digital platforms have become the new "stage." Someone can gain attention more quickly with a single viral post than with years of building a reputation in the professional space. Algorithms that regulate information traffic determine who appears on screen, who disappears, and even who is deemed credible.

Algorithm-Driven Highlights

Before the internet, reputation spread through word of mouth, print articles, or limited traditional media outlets. Today, reputation is built by automated systems that operate in seconds. Social media algorithms analyze likes, shares, and comments and then display content deemed most "relevant" or "interesting." Unfortunately, relevance doesn't always equate to quality.

For example, a doctor might become more well-known to the public not because of his research, but because of his humorous videos explaining diseases. A lawyer might become popular not because of the quality of his arguments in court, but because of his TikTok commentary on celebrity cases. This popularity isn't inherently wrong, but it poses risks when image overrides substance.

Shifting Measures of Professionalism

This phenomenon raises a serious question: is professionalism now measured by competence or by digital popularity? A true professional is still required to maintain integrity, a code of ethics, and quality of service. However, the public, exposed to algorithms, often finds it easier to trust viral figures, even if their competence is questionable.

This is what many observers call a crisis of authority. Previously, the authority of a doctor, lawyer, or academic was built on education, experience, and institutional recognition. Now, authority is often perceived through the number of followers on social media. As a result, professionals face dual pressures: maintaining the quality of their work while simultaneously addressing the demands of maintaining a digital presence.

Opportunities and Risks

Not all of these changes are bad. The spotlight of algorithms also presents significant opportunities. Adaptive professionals can leverage social media to educate the public, expand their influence, and even drive social change. Many doctors have successfully provided accurate health information amidst a sea of misinformation. Many lawyers are using digital platforms to provide legal education to the general public.

But that opportunity always comes with risks. Too much scrutiny can lead to a loss of privacy, being drawn into controversy, or being tempted to prioritize sensation over substance. Herein lies the real battle: how to remain professional amidst a stage that values virality over value.

New Awareness Needed

This era demands a new ethical awareness. Professionals can no longer turn a blind eye to social media, claiming it's "not my domain." Like it or not, every profession now lives under the scrutiny of algorithms. The question is no longer whether a professional wants to appear on social media, but how they present themselves in a way that aligns with the code of ethics, integrity, and dignity of their profession.

Therefore, understanding algorithms and how they work is not just a technological issue, but also a moral one. A professional who understands algorithmic logic can determine boundaries: what can be shared and what should be protected; how to build a positive image without sacrificing truth; and how to use the algorithm's spotlight for good, not just empty popularity.

An Algorithm Driven World

Nearly every aspect of our lives today is determined by algorithms: from what news we read, who appears on our timelines, to the recommendations for restaurants or doctors that appear in search results. We may not realize it, but algorithms have become the gateway to societal perception.

For professionals, this means that reputation is no longer solely the result of actual hard work, but also the result of what digital systems "choose" to display. Algorithms filter millions of pieces of information and determine what is deemed relevant. As a result, a professional can be "elevated" or "overlooked" not so much by the quality of their work as by uncontrollable algorithmic patterns.

Positive Impact: New Opportunities

While it may seem scary, algorithmic spotlights also bring many benefits.

Wide access to the public Doctors can spread health education to millions of people, not just to patients in the office.

Building a professional image Lawyers, academics, or consultants can demonstrate their expertise through articles, videos, or digital interviews.

Collaboration opportunitiesA positive digital footprint opens up opportunities for cross-professional and cross-national collaboration.

In other words, algorithms provide a new platform that was previously unavailable. If used wisely, this spotlight can strengthen the integrity of the profession while providing tangible benefits to society.

Negative Impact: Lurking Risks

However, algorithm highlights also harbor dangers that should not be underestimated:

Popularity replaces substance Often viral content is more appreciated than true and in-depth content.

The pressure to perform constantly Professionals feel they have to be "present" all the time, sacrificing their primary focus on work.

Reputational risk One post that is deemed wrong can destroy trust that has been built over years.

Algorithmic bias Digital systems can favor certain content not because of quality, but because of market preferences, clicks, or even hidden discrimination.

Real Case Study

The case of the influencer doctorA pediatrician in Southeast Asia has gone viral for his health education TikTok videos. The content has attracted many new patients, but he has also been criticized by colleagues for being too "entertaining" and neglecting medical communication etiquette.

Public figure lawyer case: A lawyer is better known for his legal commentary on talk shows and social media, to the point that some people consider him a "legal celebrity" rather than a legal practitioner. His popularity helps his brand, but also raises questions about his objectivity.

These two examples show that algorithms can change people's perceptions of who is considered competent.

What Can Professionals Do?

To face the algorithm era, there are several practical steps that can be used as initial guidelines:

Get to know the relevant platforms Not all social media platforms are suitable for all professions. Doctors might focus on Instagram or YouTube for visual education, while lawyers or academics might be better suited to LinkedIn or digital articles.

Understand professional ethics as a fence Before creating content, ask yourself: does it comply with the code of ethics? Could it harm patients/clients? Will it degrade the profession?

Build image consistency Don't just chase virality, but make sure the message you build aligns with your professional values.

Learning algorithm literacy Professionals don't need to be tech experts, but at least understand how basic algorithms work so they don't get trapped.

Separate personal and professional Personal life may be present in the digital space, but don't let it drown out your professional identity.

Reflections for Professionals

The algorithmic era is like a large stage with an unstoppable spotlight. Anyone who enters it must be prepared to be seen, evaluated, and even judged. But this spotlight isn't always a bad thing; it can be a tool if managed intelligently, or a trap if allowed to take control.

True professionals are required not only to appear competent, but to remain truly competent behind the scenes. Popularity may come, but integrity must never be lost. That's the key to surviving in this new era of the spotlight.

The era of algorithms has brought a new spotlight that professionals cannot escape. Reputations are now determined not only by competence and integrity in the practice room, courtroom, or lecture hall, but also by how algorithms present themselves on the public screen. Popularity can accelerate recognition, but it can also obscure substance and undermine the dignity of the profession if not accompanied by ethical awareness.

The essence of this chapter is: professionals shouldn't reject the spotlight of algorithms, but they should learn to manage it wisely. Social media and digital platforms aren't just entertainment spaces; for professions directly related to the public interest, they represent a new platform for building trust.

Therefore, every professional needs to:

Understanding algorithm logicso as not to get caught up in the illusion of popularity.

Making the code of ethics a fence, so that the spotlight does not shift the integrity value.

Using digital space as a means of education and contribution, not just self-promotion.

Maintaining a consistent professional image, because public trust is the main capital of the profession.

With this awareness, lawyers, doctors, academics, and other professionals can remain steadfast even under the spotlight of algorithms. The spotlight isn't a threat, but rather an opportunity to demonstrate that integrity remains relevant even in this viral era.

CHAPTER 2

Between Profession and Popularity

Professional Dignity as a Foundation

Every profession is born from a noble calling. A doctor promises to protect the health of patients without discrimination. A lawyer swears to uphold the law and defend justice. An academic dedicates himself to the pursuit of scientific truth. This dignity is not only personal but also social: society places special trust in professions because they are believed to hold higher moral standards.

But now, in the era of social media, that dignity is being tested by the lure of popularity. In a world governed by algorithms, public recognition is often more readily bestowed upon those who appear attractive and go viral, rather than those who work quietly but with dedication. This presents a major dilemma: should a professional stick to their values, or dance to the public spotlight?

Popularity: A Double-Edged Sword

Popularity isn't a bad thing. It can be a tool for expanding positive influence. Doctors who are popular on social media can reach millions of people with health messages. Lawyers who frequently appear in the media can raise public legal awareness. Academics who are active on digital platforms can make knowledge more accessible.

But popularity also carries serious risks:

Identity reductionA professional is better known as a "celebrity" than as a credible practitioner.

Perceptual bias The public trusts the number of followers more than certifications or real experience.

Commercialization of the profession Popularity drives some professionals to prioritize sponsorships, endorsements, or a glamorous image over public service.

Pressure to go viral In order to stay relevant, a professional may be tempted to create sensational content that demeans the dignity of his profession.

Everyday Dilemmas

Many professionals now face difficult questions:

Is it appropriate for a doctor to upload photos with his patients, even with permission, for educational content?

Is it permissible for a lawyer to make public comments about a case he or she is handling, even though ethics require confidentiality?

Should an academic oversimplify his research to make it more likely to go viral, even if it risks misconceptions?

These questions have no single answer. But one thing is clear: professionalism demands adherence to a code of ethics, even though the public spotlight offers a shortcut to fame.

Finding the Balance Point

It's unrealistic for a professional to completely reject popularity. The digital world has become a new arena, and the public demands involvement. Therefore, what's needed isn't to reject or give in to popularity, but to find a balance.

There are several principles that can be used as a guide:

Ethics over algorithms Never violate the professional code of ethics for the sake of virality.

Image as a mirror of quality Build popularity from the substance of your work, not the other way around.

Educational content is more important Make public attention a means of benefit, not just entertainment.

AuthenticityPopularity built on falsehood quickly crumbles; integrity is the long-term foundation.

True professionalism doesn't mean rejecting the digital stage, but rather embracing popularity as a tool, not an end in itself. In this way, public scrutiny doesn't undermine the dignity of the profession, but rather strengthens it.

Professional Dignity as a Foundation

Professions have always been founded on public trust. This trust arises because the public believes a doctor, lawyer, or academic is not solely seeking profit, but prioritizes moral responsibility. When a doctor treats a patient, they are not only using medical knowledge but also upholding an ethical promise: "do no harm." When a lawyer defends a client, they are not only relying on legal expertise but also upholding the principle of justice.

But in the age of social media, this dignity is threatened with erosion. The public spotlight is more easily directed to those who attract attention, rather than those with the most integrity. Popularity has become a kind of "new currency," and professionals who don't engage in the digital space risk being deemed irrelevant.

Popularity: A Double-Edged Sword

Popularity can bring extraordinary benefits: expanding influence, opening public access to knowledge, and even inspiring others. But it can also be a poison that slowly eats away at professionalism.

Positive impact:

Health education reaches millions of people.

Legal literacy is increasing thanks to simple explanations on social media.

Science can penetrate non-academic circles.

Negative impact:

Professionals are reduced to “social media artists”.

The emergence of clickbait that simplifies complex issues.

Reliance on “likes” makes professionals lose their independence of thought.

The Psychology of Popularity

To understand this dilemma, we need to touch on a bit of psychology. Popularity triggers dopamine, the same brain chemical activated when someone receives a reward or praise. This is why social media notifications can be addictive. Even professionals can fall into this trap: initially intending to educate, they end up chasing validation.

In other words, popularity is not just a social phenomenon, but also a biological one. Understanding this makes us more aware: popularity is an addiction, and only ethical discipline can provide an antidote.

Strategy to Maintain Balance

So that readers can be smarter in facing this dilemma, there are several practical strategies that can be applied:

Define digital goals from the start Is your social media presence for education, professional promotion, or simply sharing inspiration? A clear purpose will prevent you from being swept away by false popularity.

Use the "3S" principle:

Substance: every content must have knowledge or enlightenment value.

Sensitivity: avoid violating the privacy of patients, clients, or other parties.

Sustainability: content must be sustainable in the long term, not just a momentary sensation.

Separate personal and professional identities It's natural for a doctor to want to share a hobby, or a lawyer to share their family life. However, professional accounts should stay focused on their core message to avoid compromising credibility.

Periodic self-evaluation Ask yourself: "Does my content reflect my professional values, or is it just a pursuit of popularity?" If the answer leans toward the latter, it's time to rethink it.

Use popularity as a gateway, not an end goal. Popularity may be a vehicle to reach the public, but the ultimate goal remains service, education, and integrity.

Real Case Reflection

Influencer doctor: A doctor went viral for creating comedic educational videos. He succeeded in getting young people to care more about their health. However, some of his colleagues considered his approach too lighthearted and risked diminishing the prestige of the profession. This case highlights the importance of weighing communication style against professional ethics.

Celebrity lawyer: A lawyer frequently appears on television and social media commenting on sensitive cases. His popularity soars, but some people believe he's more about chasing the camera than defending the law. The lesson is clear: public scrutiny can strengthen, but it can also destroy, trust.

The dilemma between profession and popularity is the greatest challenge of the algorithmic era. Popularity is not the enemy, but neither is it the goal. It should be viewed as a means to expand positive influence, not the sole measure of success.

The key lies in balance: how to stay relevant in the digital space without losing professional dignity. Popularity may come and go, but dignity is lost once and is difficult to regain.

Practical Guide: The Middle Way for Professionals

Rather than being caught in a binary choice between maintaining one's dignity or pursuing professional popularity, a wise middle ground can be taken: using popularity to strengthen one's profession, not replace it.

Here are some strategies you can follow:

1. Build a Healthy Digital Identity

Use a professional profile photo and bio.

List primary expertise (e.g., "pediatrician" or "human rights lawyer").

Avoid nicknames or content that belittles your own profession.

2. Implement "Digital Publication Ethics"

Before posting something, ask yourself three simple things:

Is this true?(not misleading or half-informed)

Was this helpful?(add value to the public, not just to yourself)

Is this appropriate?(does not damage the dignity of the profession or violate the privacy of others)

3. Set Content Proportion

Think of your professional account like a magazine:

60% educational content (knowledge, tips, useful information)

20% inspirational content (true stories, relevant personal experiences)

20% light content (interaction, entertainment, human side that remains polite)

4. Manage Interactions Wisely

Popularity will bring a lot of comments, criticism, and even attacks. Don't be easily provoked. True professionals demonstrate their quality precisely through how they respond to the public.

5. Maintain Digital Mental Health

Set time limits for social media. Don't let "likes" and "shares" control your self-esteem. Remember: true validation comes from integrity in your work, not numbers on a screen.

Illustration: Professional Popularity Pyramid

Think of popularity as a pyramid:

BaseIntegrity & Competence (irreplaceable foundation)

Middle Layer Public Education (useful & communicative content)

Top Layer Popularity (bonus, not goal)

The biggest mistake is to invert the pyramid: put popularity at the bottom and build identity on top. Such a structure will quickly collapse.

True professionals use popularity as a bridge to connect with the public, without compromising their integrity. With practical guidance and ethical awareness, every professional can emerge on the algorithmic stage without compromising their dignity.

The dilemma between upholding professional dignity and pursuing public attention ultimately comes down to priorities. Fame may open doors, but it's dignity that keeps them open. Fame may bring thousands of people, but only integrity keeps them trusting and staying.

Many professionals fail not because they lack intelligence, but because they misplace their focus: they're too busy chasing attention to maintain their values. In the face of the rapid flow of algorithms, the public values those who are consistent, authentic, and loyal to their code of ethics.

The key is to change your perspective:

Popularity should not be a goal, but a tool.

The public spotlight should not be used as a platform for ego, but as a channel for devotion.

Social media should not just be a place to show off, but a space to share values and knowledge.

If this principle is upheld, a lawyer can build legal awareness without losing authority, a doctor can reach more patients without degrading medical dignity, and an academic can disseminate knowledge without sacrificing scientific credibility.

Thus, profession and popularity need not be at odds. The two can coexist, as long as professionals are willing to use dignity as an anchor and popularity as merely a screen.

Ultimately, the question we should be asking is not "How popular am I today?" but "Is my popularity providing any real benefit, and am I still true to the integrity of the profession?"

The most crucial thing to remember is: popularity is temporary, but professional reputation is long-term. Public attention may fluctuate with algorithmic trends, but good name and integrity will remain, even after the algorithm changes.

For a doctor, lawyer, or other professional, reputation isn't built on the number of followers, but on the consistency of carrying out professional duties. The world may know you more quickly through social media, but it can also forget you more quickly if professional values are sacrificed for the sake of sensationalism.

That is why, every step in the digital space must always be based on a simple question:

"Does this make me more respected as a professional, or just more known as a temporary celebrity?"

The honest answer to that question will determine whether you are building a sustainable career or simply enjoying a momentary moment in the spotlight.

CHAPTER 3

Algorithms and Image Illusions

An Algorithm Controlled World

In the digital age, we no longer have complete control over what we see. Every time we open social media, algorithms are silently at work: sorting, filtering, and then displaying content that they believe is most relevant or interesting to us.

Interestingly, algorithms not only determine what we see, but also how we perceive others. A person's popularity, credibility, and even professional reputation can now be shaped or distorted by algorithms.

A doctor can appear highly credible simply because their content frequently appears on the homepage. A lawyer can appear powerful because they frequently appear on trending topics. However, the truth doesn't always align with what the algorithm "promotes."

The Mechanism of Image Illusion

There are several ways algorithms create the illusion of images:

Repetition Effect

The more frequently someone appears, the greater the chance that the public will consider them credible even if they do not necessarily have the same quality.

Numbers as Symbols of Authority The number of followers, likes, and shares is often considered a measure of competence. However, these numbers can be manipulated, or simply reflect popularity, not quality.

Filter Bubble Algorithms tend to display content that aligns with user preferences. As a result, someone can appear "widely agreed upon" when they're actually only viral in a limited circle.

Sensational Content Overrides Substance Content with provocative titles or a dramatic style is more often promoted by the algorithm than calm, educational content.

Impact on Professionals

For professionals, this mechanism brings major challenges:

Fake reputation: someone can appear to be an expert because they are popular, even though they don't necessarily have the capacity.

Unfair competition: professionals who are serious about maintaining ethics and substance often lose out to those who are good at playing algorithms.

Pressure to be sensational: there is a great temptation to sacrifice depth for viral speed.

However, behind the risk lies an opportunity: algorithms can be a tool for spreading value if used wisely.

Strategies for Dealing with the Illusion of Algorithms

To avoid getting caught up in a false reputation, there are several steps you can take:

Build Content with Substance Algorithms may love sensationalism, but the long-term public values consistency and depth.

Use Numbers as a Mirror, Not a Goal Likes and shares can be indicators of reach, but they should not be used as a measure of self-worth or credibility.

Diversifying Digital Presence Don't rely solely on one platform. Write articles, appear on official forums, or participate in online academic discussions so your reputation isn't entirely dependent on social media algorithms.

Stick to Ethics Not everything the "algorithm asks" needs to be followed. It's better to lose a viral opportunity than lose your dignity.

Algorithms are machines without conscience. They only seek attention, not truth. Therefore, professionals must be more discerning: don't let algorithms be the sole arbiters of reputation.

True reputation isn't what you see on screen, but what you believe in when the screen goes off. Popularity can be deceiving, but integrity can never be faked.

In the digital age, we no longer have complete control over what we see. Every time we open social media, algorithms are silently at work:

sorting, filtering, and then displaying content that they believe is most relevant or interesting to us. Algorithms are designed to hold users' attention for as long as possible, not to ensure the truthfulness or depth of content.

Interestingly, algorithms not only determine what we see, but also how we perceive others. A person's popularity, credibility, and even professional reputation can now be shaped or distorted by algorithms.

A doctor can appear highly credible simply because their content frequently appears on the homepage. A lawyer can appear powerful because they frequently appear on trending topics. However, the truth doesn't always align with what the algorithm promotes.

The Mechanism of Image Illusion

First, the repetition effect. The more frequently someone appears, the more likely the public is to perceive them as credible. Repeated appearances create the perception of expertise, even if the message is simplistic or even misleading.

Second, numbers as a symbol of authority. The number of followers, comments, and likes is often seen as proof of greatness. However, numbers can be bought, manipulated, or simply reflect personal appeal, not competence.

Third, filter bubbles. Algorithms create information bubbles that make us see only content relevant to our interests. If a professional is popular in one community, they can appear to dominate the discourse, even if they're unknown in other circles.

Fourth, sensational content trumps substance. Algorithms favor content that quickly triggers emotions, whether laughter, anger, or admiration. As a result, in-depth, educational content is often buried by more dramatic content.

Impact on Professionals

For professionals, this mechanism presents significant challenges. A false reputation can develop quickly. Someone with little experience could be considered a reference simply because their video went viral.

Conversely, experienced professionals can lose the spotlight if they don't actively produce content.

Competition also becomes unfair. Doctors or lawyers who adhere to ethical standards may be reluctant to create bombastic content, while those who dare to push the boundaries may quickly become known. Pressure to follow the hype arises. There's a strong incentive to create content that conforms to the algorithm's preferences, even if it goes against the dignity of the profession.

However, algorithms are not just threats. If properly understood, they can be a bridge. Algorithms can help disseminate enlightening information, improve legal and health literacy, or expand public access to scientific knowledge.

Real Example

A dentist in Indonesia once became popular for creating educational videos about dental care in a lighthearted and humorous style. He managed to reach millions of people who were previously reluctant to listen to health information. His popularity didn't diminish his dignity, as he stuck to medical facts.

Conversely, there's also the case of a health influencer who went viral for promoting a therapy without scientific basis. Her videos were viewed millions of times, but she was later reprimanded by a professional association for misleading the public. The false reputation built by the algorithm ultimately collapsed when the truth was tested.

Strategies for Dealing with the Illusion of Algorithms

There are several steps you can take to avoid falling into the false image trap.

First, create content with substance. It might not go viral immediately, but it will have a long-term impact.

Second, use numbers as a mirror, not a goal. They can provide a sense of reach, but they shouldn't be used as a determinant of self-worth.

Third, diversify your digital presence. Don't just be present on social media, where algorithms are subject to change. Publish articles in journals, speak in official forums, or participate in academic discussions. This way, your reputation isn't solely driven by algorithms.

Fourth, stick to ethics. Not everything the algorithm asks for needs to be fulfilled. It's better to lose a viral opportunity than lose your dignity.

Fifth, build long-term authority. Investing in expertise, research, and tangible work will lay the foundation for a reputation that can't be undermined by changing digital trends.

Algorithms are machines without conscience. They only seek attention, not truth. Therefore, professionals must be more discerning: don't let algorithms be the sole arbiters of reputation.

True reputation isn't what you see on screen, but what you believe in when the screen goes off. Popularity can be deceiving, but integrity can never be faked.

In the digital age, we no longer have complete control over what we see. Every time we open social media, algorithms are silently at work: sorting, filtering, and then displaying content that they believe is most relevant or interesting to us. Algorithms are designed to hold users' attention for as long as possible, not to ensure the truthfulness or depth of content.

Interestingly, algorithms not only determine what we see, but also how we perceive others. A person's popularity, credibility, and even professional reputation can now be shaped or distorted by algorithms.

A doctor can appear highly credible simply because their content frequently appears on the homepage. A lawyer can appear powerful because they frequently appear on trending topics. However, the truth doesn't always align with what the algorithm promotes.

The Mechanism of Image Illusion

First, the repetition effect. The more frequently someone appears, the more likely the public is to perceive them as credible. Repeated appearances create the perception of expertise, even if the message is simplistic or even misleading.

Second, numbers as a symbol of authority. The number of followers, comments, and likes is often seen as proof of greatness. However, numbers can be bought, manipulated, or simply reflect personal appeal, not competence.

Third, filter bubbles. Algorithms create information bubbles that make us see only content relevant to our interests. If a professional is popular in one community, they can appear to dominate the discourse, even if they're unknown in other circles.

Fourth, sensational content trumps substance. Algorithms favor content that quickly triggers emotions, whether laughter, anger, or admiration. As a result, in-depth, educational content is often buried by more dramatic content.

Impact on Professionals

For professionals, this mechanism presents significant challenges. A false reputation can develop quickly. Someone with little experience could be considered a reference simply because their video went viral. Conversely, experienced professionals can lose the spotlight if they don't actively produce content.

Competition also becomes unfair. Doctors or lawyers who adhere to ethical standards may be reluctant to create bombastic content, while those who dare to push the boundaries may quickly become known. Pressure to follow the hype arises. There's a strong incentive to create content that conforms to the algorithm's preferences, even if it goes against the dignity of the profession.

However, algorithms are not just threats. If properly understood, they can be a bridge. Algorithms can help disseminate enlightening information, improve legal and health literacy, or expand public access to scientific knowledge.

Real Example

A dentist in Indonesia once became popular for creating educational videos about dental care in a lighthearted and humorous style. He managed to reach millions of people who were previously reluctant to listen to health information. His popularity didn't diminish his dignity, as he stuck to medical facts.

Conversely, there's also the case of a health influencer who went viral for promoting a therapy without scientific basis. Her videos were viewed millions of times, but she was later reprimanded by a professional association for misleading the public. The false reputation built by the algorithm ultimately collapsed when the truth was tested.

Skills That Professionals Need to Master

To counter the illusion of algorithms, professionals cannot rely solely on substantive expertise. A number of additional skills are now essential:

1. Digital literacy: Understanding how algorithms, platforms, and people's content consumption patterns work.
2. Public communication: Able to convey complex messages in simple language without losing the essence.
3. Reputation management: Recognizing that every digital footprint shapes a long-term image.
4. Digital ethics: Defining clear boundaries between education, entertainment, and self-promotion to avoid violating ethical codes.
5. Emotional intelligence: Not easily tempted by momentary popularity, remains calm when facing criticism or negative comments.

Practical Tips for Professionals

To be more concrete, here are the steps that can be put into practice.

1. Determine the main goal before creating content: whether it

is for education, clarification, or sharing insights.

2. Use language that is easy to understand without belittling the complexity of the science.
3. Don't get hung up on numbers. Focus on the quality of your interactions with your audience.
4. Document professional achievements in formal spaces, such as publications, seminars, or certifications, so that your reputation doesn't depend solely on social media.
5. Regularly evaluate yourself: are your digital activities aligned with the dignity of your profession or are they starting to shift towards mere entertainment.

Algorithms are machines without conscience. They only seek attention, not truth. Therefore, professionals must be more discerning: don't let algorithms be the sole arbiters of reputation.

True reputation isn't what you see on screen, but what you believe in when the screen goes off. Popularity can be deceiving, but integrity can never be faked.

CHAPTER 4

A Brief History of Professional Codes of Ethics

Every profession that directly impacts human life is bound by moral values and social responsibility. Codes of ethics are not meant to be mere decoration, but rather as guidelines to ensure that professions are carried out for the benefit of the wider community, not merely for personal gain. To understand the urgency of codes of ethics in the digital age, we need to look back at their long history.

Origin: Hippocratic Oath

In the world of medicine, one of the most important milestones is the Hippocratic Oath, which originated in ancient Greece around the 5th century BC. Hippocrates, known as the Father of Medicine, emphasized that a physician must maintain patient confidentiality, not abuse his expertise to harm, and always prioritize the patient's well-being. While the language and context are ancient, the basic principles remain in use today.

The Hippocratic Oath demonstrates that, from the outset, professions that concern human life require moral boundaries. Knowledge and skill can be a double-edged sword: healing or harm. Ethics exist to ensure that sword is used properly.

Developments in the Middle Ages

While religion played a central role in both Europe and the Islamic world, the principles of professional ethics were often linked to spiritual teachings. In Islamic tradition, for example, the works of scholars like Ibn Sina and Al-Razi addressed not only medical science but also emphasized the morals of a healer. A professional was viewed as a trusted servant of God, not merely a technical worker.

In the legal field, ethical developments were also evident. European jurists established professional traditions that bound lawyers to maintain client confidentiality and avoid conflicts of interest. In the

Islamic world, qadis (judges) and muftis (muftis) were required to be fair because they were trusted to carry the voice of God's law.

Modern Era: Written Code of Ethics

As the 19th and 20th centuries approached, various professions began to formulate written codes of ethics. Medical associations in the United Kingdom and the United States, for example, created official documents outlining doctors' obligations to patients, colleagues, and the public.

Likewise, the legal profession. In 1908, the American Bar Association (ABA) adopted the Canons of Professional Ethics, which later evolved into the Model Rules of Professional Conduct. Its goal was clear: to ensure the legal profession remains a pillar of justice, not simply a means of earning a living.

Other professions have followed suit. Accountants, architects, psychologists, and even journalists have developed their own codes of ethics. The bottom line is the same: maintaining public trust by placing the public interest above personal gain.

Code of Ethics in Indonesia

In Indonesia, professional codes of ethics have also evolved alongside modernization. The Indonesian Medical Association (IDI) has an Indonesian Code of Medical Ethics that emphasizes confidentiality, professionalism, and patient interests. The Indonesian Advocates Association (PERADI) has an Advocates Code of Ethics that regulates integrity, confidentiality, and prohibits abuse of the profession.

This code of ethics is not just a formal rule, but also a tool to maintain public trust in the profession. Without trust, a profession that concerns life, justice, or a person's future will lose legitimacy.

Relevance in the Digital Age

This long history demonstrates that codes of ethics are nothing new. However, the challenges of the digital age are different. While the primary challenge once was maintaining patient confidentiality or avoiding conflicts of interest, a new challenge now arises: how to maintain the dignity of the profession amidst public scrutiny, algorithms, and social media.

A doctor can now be better known for viral content than for his work in a hospital. A lawyer can rise to prominence more quickly through a sensational interview than through the quality of his or her defense in court. Modern codes of ethics must address this issue: how the profession remains rooted in the value of integrity, even as the digital platform offers the lure of instant fame.

The history of ethical codes teaches us one important lesson: any profession that concerns human interests cannot be separated from moral responsibility. From the Hippocratic Oath to modern codes of ethics, the guiding principle remains the same: upholding the dignity of the profession and protecting the public.

Today, the challenge is no longer just maintaining ethics in physical practice spaces, but also in the digital realm. Professional ethics must remain a compass guiding professionals so they don't get lost in the illusion of algorithms.

Code of Ethics Above Algorithms

If history shows that codes of ethics have always been born from the need to maintain the dignity of the profession, then today's challenge is to ensure that codes of ethics remain of higher value than the spotlight of algorithms.

Algorithms operate based on attention calculations. They prioritize what quickly attracts attention, not what is true. In contrast, codes of ethics operate based on moral values and integrity. They prioritize what is useful and true, even if it isn't always popular.

This is what distinguishes a true professional from a mere public figure. True professionals measure themselves by ethical standards, not by the number of views or followers. Popularity can be a bonus, but it's not the goal. If popularity is achieved at the expense of ethics, then it's no longer an achievement, but a betrayal of the profession.

Why Should the Code of Ethics Be Number One?

First, a code of ethics protects public trust. Without ethics, doctors can become drug dealers, lawyers can become legal manipulators, and journalists can become sensationalists. Lost trust is difficult to restore.

Second, a code of ethics provides identity and legitimacy. A profession is recognized by society not because of the popularity of its members, but because of the assurance that they adhere to clear moral standards.

Third, a code of ethics serves as a personal safeguard. In an era where the temptation to go viral is so great, a code of ethics serves as a reminder that not every opportunity is worth taking, not every stage is worth stepping on, and not every attention is worth the professional pride.

Ethics as a Digital Compass

A doctor creating health education content should ask: is this information accurate, scientifically sound, and not misleading? A lawyer appearing in the media should ask: does this commentary maintain client confidentiality and not undermine the dignity of the law?

These simple questions are how to ensure ethics always serve as a compass. Popularity may come or go, but integrity must remain steadfast.

From Hippocrates to modern codes of ethics, we have learned that professions can only survive if they are founded on ethical foundations. Now, as algorithms attempt to dictate what is visible and what is not, true professionals must boldly assert: algorithms are tools, not arbiters of value.

A code of ethics must be upheld, as it serves as a boundary that protects the dignity of the profession and public trust. Without ethics, popularity is merely illusory. With ethics, reputation is eternal.

Real Case: When Ethics Are Tested in the Algorithmic Era

In recent years, we've witnessed an interesting and worrying phenomenon. A doctor can suddenly become famous by creating educational content on social media. While much of this is beneficial, some are tempted to create dramatic, sensationalized content, even oversimplifying diseases for the sake of "likes" and "shares." This is where ethics come into play. Is it permissible for a professional to manipulate the facts for the sake of going viral?

In the legal world, many lawyers appear in the media not to explain the facts of a case, but rather to build their own image. What should be objective comments can turn into personal attacks or public opinion-driven misinformation. After all, clients and legal proceedings must be kept confidential. Algorithms may push controversial comments to go viral faster, but ethical standards demand caution and dignity.

Even in journalism, we often see news stories cut and cut for clickbait. While speed may attract readers, it often comes at the expense of completeness.

The lesson from these cases is clear: algorithms provide instant rewards, but ethical codes safeguard the profession. Viral may last a day, but a professional reputation must be maintained for life.

Affirming Priorities: Ethics Over Algorithms

The long history of codes of ethics, coupled with the realities of the digital age, teaches that professions should not be subject to algorithmic logic. A profession is not a stage for entertainment, but rather a trust that demands integrity.

While algorithms offer shortcuts to popularity, codes of ethics remind us that not all shortcuts are worth taking. It is precisely in rejecting these shortcuts that a professional's dignity is tested.

When a doctor chooses to maintain patient confidentiality even though revealing it could go viral, he or she is putting ethics above algorithms. When a lawyer refrains from controversial comments that could boost his or her popularity, he or she is proving that the dignity of his or her profession is more important than media scrutiny.

Building a Culture of Digital Ethics

Going forward, the challenges will become increasingly complex. The younger generation of professionals was born alongside social media. For them, sharing and appearing in public spaces is second nature. Therefore, it is crucial to build a new culture: professional digital ethics.

This culture doesn't prohibit professionals from being present on social media. On the contrary, their presence is crucial to ensure the public doesn't receive information from unreliable sources. However, this culture demands that this presence be framed by a code of ethics. Information may be popular, but it must remain accurate. Content can be lighthearted, but it must not be misleading. Public scrutiny is welcome, but the dignity of the profession must not be compromised.

The history of professional codes of ethics is not merely a record of the past. It is evidence that, for thousands of years, humans have always needed moral barriers to distinguish service from commerce, calling from mere work, and honor from mere popularity.

In the digital age, this safeguard is increasingly important. Algorithms operate without conscience; they only calculate what's preferred, not what's right. If professionals surrender completely to the logic of algorithms, the profession will lose its direction and dignity.

However, this is where a professional's true strength lies. They are able to stand their ground, using a code of ethics as a guiding compass, not merely an accessory. Popularity may attract admiration, but integrity is what inspires trust.

History teaches us lessons, and the times present us challenges. Now we have a choice: do we let algorithms define our image, or do we uphold ethics as a more solid foundation?

The answer to this question will determine whether professions in the algorithmic era will become mere fads or remain enduring pillars of public trust.

And one thing to remember: algorithms can elevate a reputation, but only ethics can keep it honorable. Because ultimately, technology may change, the public spotlight may shift, but a commitment to a code of ethics is the one legacy that never goes out of style.

CHAPTER 5

Profession as a Calling

A true profession is born not merely from skill, but from a calling to serve. A doctor works not only to prescribe medicine, but to care for life. A lawyer works not merely to cite legal articles, but to uphold justice. An educator works not only to teach a subject, but to shape the future. This is what distinguishes a profession from mere employment: a moral calling.

Responsibility as a Foundation

Every profession is born out of a social contract with society. The public entrusts professionals with their health, justice, education, and information. Therefore, responsibility is a non-negotiable foundation. Doctors bear responsibility for the lives of their patients, lawyers for the fate of their clients, and journalists for the accuracy of the information they convey. Without responsibility, professions lose their social legitimacy.

Integrity as Identity

Integrity is the consistency between words, knowledge, and actions. Amidst the scrutiny of algorithms, integrity ensures a professional isn't tempted to manipulate facts simply for popularity. Integrity allows a doctor to say "I don't know" when there's no scientific evidence. Integrity prevents a lawyer from resorting to dirty tricks even when the odds seem strong. Integrity also keeps an educator objective even when faced with social pressure.

Service as a Goal

The essence of a profession is not to pursue personal gain, but to benefit others. This service is what makes a profession noble. A doctor feels called to help, not simply to earn an honorarium. A lawyer feels called to fight for justice, not merely to win a case. When service is the central orientation, the dignity of the profession will always be maintained, even when shaken by the dynamics of the times.

Profession is not just a career

For many, work is a way to earn a living. However, for a true professional, their profession is part of their identity. They are not just what they do, but who they are. Therefore, a true professional is willing to turn down lucrative opportunities if they conflict with their ethics. They realize that maintaining the dignity of their profession is far more important than simply adding to their bank account.

Professions in the Algorithmic Era

The biggest challenge in the digital age is how to maintain a profession as a calling, not a platform. Algorithms encourage people to show up, speak out, and stand out. There's nothing wrong with being present in the public sphere, but a major mistake occurs when professionals sacrifice their ethical calling for the sake of a momentary spotlight.

A doctor who compromises the quality of his services because he's busy creating content is an example of a loss of direction. A lawyer who is more focused on building a media image than on delving into clients' cases is a sign that the profession has been reduced to mere show.

Ultimately, a profession is not a career chosen solely for its rewards, but rather a calling that demands loyalty. Responsibility is its foundation, integrity is its identity, and service is its ultimate goal.

Algorithms may shape fleeting perceptions of who's popular, but only loyalty to one's profession will establish a true reputation. A true profession thrives not on the spotlight, but on dedication.

Differentiating between Job, Career, and Profession

To better understand the nature of a profession, it is important to distinguish between three terms that are often used interchangeably: job, career, and profession.

- **Work**is an activity carried out to earn income. The focus is on livelihood.
- **Career**is a person's ups and downs in a particular field, usually

seen from the position, title or achievements attained.

- **Profession**It transcends both. It's not just about income or position, but about moral calling, devotion, and social responsibility.

By understanding this difference, a doctor or lawyer will realize that their profession is not just a means to a comfortable life, but a means to serve society.

Characteristics of a True Profession

To make it clearer, let's look at some of the characteristics of a true profession:

1. **Scientific Basis**Professions are based on in-depth knowledge gained from long education.
2. **Code of Ethics**There are binding moral rules so that expertise is not misused.
3. **Public Responsibility**Profession is not only for personal interests, but for the interests of the wider community.
4. **The Sublime Call**There is an inner motivation that drives a person to remain true to values, despite the temptation of profit or popularity.

Keeping these characteristics in mind, a professional can evaluate himself: is he still pursuing his profession as a calling, or is he simply turning it into an image tool?

Reflective Practice for Professionals

To be more applicable, here are some reflective questions that can be used as material for personal evaluation:

- Are the decisions I make driven more by professional ethics or by the desire to appear popular?
- Am I willing to forfeit economic opportunities or public attention in order to maintain professional integrity?

- Is my service truly helping others, or just adding to my image in the digital space?

Answering these questions honestly can help a professional return to the essence of his profession.

Living the Profession as a Calling in the Digital Age

Living one's profession as a calling in the age of algorithms requires balance. Professionals shouldn't be anti-technology, but they shouldn't completely submit to algorithmic logic either. Social media, for example, can be a tremendous educational tool if used responsibly. However, it can become a trap if used solely to seek false recognition.

The key is to always put responsibility, integrity, and service above popularity. That way, technology won't control professionals, but rather the opposite: ethical professionals will be able to harness technology for noble purposes.

A profession is a calling that demands more than mere expertise. It demands a loyal heart, a clear mind, and a commitment to the public interest. True professionals are not those who receive the most attention, but rather those who consistently uphold their values even when the spotlight turns away.

Algorithms can accelerate fame, but only responsibility, integrity, and service can make a professional remembered with respect.

Psychological Dimensions in Professional Calling

A professional calling doesn't emerge by chance. It arises from the intersection of one's abilities, societal needs, and inner drive. In modern psychology, calling is often associated with the concept of meaningful work. People who pursue their calling not only seek income but also find inner satisfaction from feeling that their lives matter to others.

According to Viktor Frankl, the psychologist renowned for his logotherapy, humans seek not only happiness but also meaning. In a professional context, meaning is the fuel that fuels resilience in the face of pressure, temptation, and even risk. A doctor remains willing to work night shifts not solely for the paycheck, but because he finds meaning in saving lives. A lawyer remains steadfast in defending justice despite the pressures of power, knowing that his profession is a calling greater than mere profit.

Psychology of Altruism and Empathy

Professional calling is also closely related to altruism, the human tendency to care for the well-being of others. True professionals possess a high level of empathy, allowing them to feel the suffering or needs of others as if they were their own. This empathy is what allows a doctor to see patients not merely as "medical cases" but as human beings in need of emotional support. Empathy is also what keeps a teacher patient in educating a difficult student, or a lawyer persistently fighting for the rights of the marginalized.

When empathy and altruism combine with professional skill, a holistic service is born: not only healing the body, but also strengthening the soul; not only defending the law, but also restoring a sense of justice; not only teaching, but also shaping character.

Intrinsic vs. Extrinsic Motivation

In motivational psychology, there are two main human drivers: extrinsic motivation (external drives, such as salary, recognition, or popularity) and intrinsic motivation (inner drives, such as personal satisfaction, meaning in life, or moral values).

Professionals who work solely for extrinsic motivation are easily swayed when rewards diminish or the spotlight shifts. However, those driven by intrinsic motivation remain committed even when praise is lacking, because what they pursue is noble values and inner satisfaction.

This is the difference between a job as a mere career and a profession as a calling. A career is easily ended when the rewards are no longer commensurate, while a calling continues even amidst hardship.

Psychology of Moral Resilience

One important aspect of understanding a profession as a calling is moral resilience. This is a professional's ability to remain steadfast in ethical values despite facing significant pressure.

A doctor in a remote area may work with minimal facilities, but he or she still provides the best possible service. A journalist may face threats for exposing the truth, but he or she remains loyal to the truth. This is proof that professional calling strengthens moral resilience: it enables one to adhere to integrity despite environmental pressures.

Viewing professions from a psychological perspective leads us to one important conclusion: a true profession is not born simply from education, degrees, or expertise, but from an inner calling that provides meaning, empathy, and moral resilience.

A profession as a calling is a bond between the individual and society, between conscience and responsibility. Algorithms may create the illusion of popularity, but only those who are true to their professional calling will be respected over time.

A true professional asks not only "what do I get out of this profession?" but also "what can I give to others through this profession?" This question is what distinguishes a calling from a mere job, and dignity from mere image.

Ultimately, a professional calling is an inexhaustible source of energy. Fame may fade, wealth may diminish, but the meaning gained from service never fades. This calling is what keeps a professional standing tall when the spotlight fades, and keeps working faithfully even without applause.

CHAPTER 6.

The Temptation of Social Media

Social media is a new space where people interact, seek information, and seek recognition. For professionals, social media can be a tool for education, reputation building, and even networking. However, behind these opportunities lies a subtle yet dangerous temptation: the desire to be liked, followed, and go viral.

The Psychology Behind "Likes"

When someone gets a "like" on their post, the brain releases dopamine, a chemical that creates feelings of pleasure and satisfaction. This effect is similar to what happens when someone receives a reward or recognition. That's why "likes" on social media are so addictive: each time we get one, our brain feels rewarded and wants to repeat it.

For professionals, this can be a double-edged sword. On the one hand, "likes" can be an indicator that a message is well-received. However, on the other hand, relying on the number of "likes" can tempt someone to adjust content for popularity, even at the expense of depth, accuracy, or even ethics.

The Psychology Behind "Followers"

The number of followers is often seen as a symbol of influence. The more followers a person has, the greater their self-confidence. In social psychology, this is called social validation, the human need to be recognized and accepted by their group.

Problems arise when a professional begins to measure their worth solely by the number of followers. Doctors may feel more valued by having hundreds of thousands of followers, while lawyers may be tempted to appear sensational to expand their audience. However, follower count doesn't always directly correlate with professional quality or the veracity of the information shared.

Pressure to Go Viral

Virality is the ultimate temptation of social media. A viral post can garner widespread attention in a short time. Psychologically, virality creates a feeling of euphoria as one feels noticed, respected, and even adored.

However, the pressure to go viral can foster a dangerous mindset. Professionals can be tempted to accelerate their popularity by making controversial statements, revealing things that should be kept private, or revealing personal aspects that are inappropriate for the public sphere.

In psychology, this is related to the phenomenon of the performance trap, a trap where someone continually performs not for a calling or value, but simply to maintain public attention. As a result, professional identity can be eroded, replaced by a digital identity that is more driven by algorithms than ethics.

A Professional's Inner Conflict

Behind all this, professionals often experience an inner conflict: the urge to meet public expectations on social media and the obligation to adhere to a code of ethics. Psychologically, this conflict is exhausting, forcing one to choose between instant popularity and long-term credibility.

Many people end up experiencing digital burnout, a mental exhaustion caused by the pressure to always be present, relevant, and in the spotlight. However, a true profession demands focus, consistency, and inner peace to serve others.

The lure of social media operates not only on a logical level, but also on a deeper psychological level: the human need for acceptance, appreciation, and praise. Likes, followers, and virality can be healthy reinforcements when used consciously, but they can become addictive when used as the primary measure of self-worth.

For a professional, this temptation can only be overcome by recognizing their true calling in their profession. Fame may come, but it should never be the goal. The true goal remains service, integrity, and responsibility.

Algorithms may flatter popularity, but sound human psychology knows that true self-esteem is born not from the number of followers, but from loyalty to professional values.

Managing Temptation: Psychological Strategies for Professionals

For social media to be a healthy tool, professionals need to understand how to manage themselves amidst the torrent of "likes" and "followers." The following strategies can help:

1. **Setting Intentions From the Start**Before posting anything, ask yourself: is my goal in sharing this to benefit others, or is it simply to get attention? Awareness of intention can be the first line of defense to ensure your content remains meaningful.
2. **Distinguishing Self-Worth from Popularity**Remember that professional value isn't determined by the number of followers. A doctor with 50,000 followers can be just as valuable as one without a social media account, as long as they adhere to a code of ethics and provide the best possible service.
3. **Using Social Media as an Educational Tool**Instead of chasing virality, use social media to disseminate true, accurate, and useful information. This way, the resulting public attention will align with professional values, not conflict with them.
4. **Implementing Digital Boundaries**Set boundaries about when, what, and how you interact on social media. Don't let social media drain your energy, time, and focus that should be used for professional service.
5. **Building a Consistent Digital Identity**Ensure your digital image aligns with your professional integrity. Don't create two faces: one professional in the real world and another sensationalist online. This consistency will strengthen public

trust.

Benefits of Managing Social Media Wisely

When professionals are able to position themselves appropriately on social media, several major benefits will be gained:

- **Increasing Educational Reach**Correct information can reach more people, so that the role of professionals in educating society is wider.
- **Building Public Trust**A consistent, ethical, and useful social media account will strengthen a long-term reputation, more than just momentary popularity.
- **Reducing Psychological Stress**By not getting caught up in the obsession of "likes" or "followers", a professional will be calmer, less anxious, and more focused on the essence of his profession.
- **Becoming a Digital Role Model**The presence of ethical professionals on social media can be a positive example for society, while also counteracting the flood of misleading information.
- **Turning Algorithms Into Partners**When the content you create is consistently useful, the algorithm will work to spread it. In other words, professionals are no longer victims of the algorithm, but instead use it for a noble purpose.

The lure of social media poses a real psychological challenge for professionals. Likes, followers, and virality tap into a deep human need: the need for recognition. However, when managed consciously, social media can be a tool to strengthen professional calling, expand service, and strengthen integrity.

A true professional doesn't measure success by the number of digital cheers, but by the real impact they have on the lives of others.

Ultimately, it's not popularity that earns respect for a profession, but rather adherence to its core values amidst the ever-changing spotlight.

Why Is This Temptation So Strong?

To understand why social media is so alluring, we need to look at it from a basic human psychology perspective. There are three fundamental needs that social media directly taps into:

1. **The need for recognition**From a young age, humans learn that appreciation makes them feel valuable. Social media reinforces this mechanism by providing instant signals in the form of "likes" or positive comments.
2. **The need for connection**Humans are social creatures. Followers give the illusion of a broad network, even if those connections are often superficial.
3. **Need for achievement**Virality is perceived as a triumph, but this apparent achievement often doesn't align with the quality of professional work.

These three needs are psychologically valid, but when directed entirely at social media, they turn into traps that lead professionals away from their true calling.

Psychological Risks of Social Media Addiction

Besides the benefits, there are real risks that professionals should be aware of:

- **Social Comparison**Seeing other colleagues go viral can create feelings of inferiority or envy, even though these achievements are not always relevant to professional quality.
- **Emotional Dependence**Moods can fluctuate depending on the number of likes or comments, so self-esteem depends on digital validation.
- **Losing Focus**Obsession with new content makes

professionals lose concentration on their main tasks, for example, a doctor is more busy making videos than delving into medical research.
- **Digital Burnout**The pressure to always be active, always relevant, and always in the spotlight can trigger mental fatigue that impacts productivity and emotional health.

Mindset Transformation: From Popularity to Usefulness

To avoid getting trapped, professionals need to change their perspective:

- Measure success not by the number of likes, but by how many people it actually helps.
- Treat followers not as a number, but as a community that can be educated.
- View virality not as a goal, but as a side effect if the content is indeed useful and valuable.

With this perspective, professionals are no longer slaves to algorithms, but leaders of narrative in the digital space.

The allure of social media is so powerful because it taps into the most fundamental aspects of the human psyche: the need for recognition, connection, and achievement. However, this allure is only dangerous if left unchecked.

True professionals need to realize that social media is just a tool, not a measure of self-worth. Likes, followers, and virality may come and go, but dedication to the profession will always be a source of true respect.

Ultimately, there's only one question worth asking before posting anything: "Does this enhance the dignity of my profession or diminish it?" An honest answer to that question will determine whether a professional is building a legacy or simply chasing a momentary moment of attention.

Real Examples from the Field

1. **The Doctor Who Went Viral for His Educational Content**An Indonesian pediatrician was once widely known for creating short educational content about infant and child health on social media. Rather than simply following entertainment trends, he consistently provided simple, practical, and ethical information. As a result, he became a reference for many parents and was trusted by the media for interviews. His popularity stemmed not from sensationalism, but from consistently providing benefits.
2. **Lawyer Caught in Controversy**On the other hand, there are lawyers who deliberately create content full of drama, exposing clients' secrets, or showcasing lavish lifestyles to attract attention. Their content may go viral, but they are later reprimanded by professional organizations for demeaning the dignity of the law. This instant popularity results in long-term reputational damage.
3. **Psychologist with Empathetic Content**A clinical psychologist created a short video about mental health during the pandemic. He wasn't chasing virality, but because his content touched people's emotional needs, thousands of people shared it. He became popular not because of algorithmic tricks, but because of the sincerity and relevance of the content to the public's needs.
4. **The Surgeon Who Lost Credibility**There was also the case of a surgeon abroad who frequently uploaded videos of himself dancing in the operating room, even while patients were on the operating table. Although the videos went viral, he received strong public criticism and was ultimately disciplined

for perceived disrespect for patients. This case demonstrates how going viral can destroy a career if it violates basic professional ethics.

Lessons from Real Cases

- Popularity can last long if it is born from values and ethics.
- Momentary virality can destroy dignity when built on sensation.
- Professionals must always consider: does this content strengthen trust or undermine it?

By recognizing this reality, professionals can learn that algorithms are merely the door, but integrity is the foundation. Without a foundation, any success will crumble as quickly as it came.

For social media to become a tool that strengthens professional dignity, several principles must be instilled in daily life. First, always start with the intention of providing benefit, not seeking attention. Second, understand that a professional's worth is not determined by the number of followers or likes, but by their dedication and integrity. Third, use social media as a platform for education and enlightenment, not as a platform for sensationalism.

A smart professional will view social media as a bridge, not a destination. Public attention may come and go, but the most valuable footprint is when people gain knowledge, hope, or solutions from what we share. With this awareness, social media is no longer a temptation, but a tool aligned with our professional calling.

Ultimately, true professionals are those who remain steadfast amidst the algorithmic tide, maintaining ethics as their compass, and refusing to succumb to the temptations of false popularity. From this comes a solid, respected, and enduring reputation.

In the real world, professional codes of ethics are clear: maintaining client or patient confidentiality, prioritizing the public interest, upholding integrity, and upholding the dignity of the profession. However, in the digital space, these principles are tested in new ways. Information can spread in seconds, opinions can go viral without verification, and the pressure to maintain a high level of performance can blur the lines between personal and professional interests.

Ethics in cyberspace are not new rules replacing classical ethics, but rather an extension of existing principles. What changes is the medium, not the underlying values. Professionals are still required to maintain confidentiality, honesty, objectivity, and respect for human dignity.

Ethical Challenges in the Digital Age

1. Confidentiality at Risk: Photos, recordings, or conversations can easily be leaked when shared carelessly. A doctor who posts a patient's case without permission, even for educational purposes, could be violating both ethics and the law.
2. The Boundary Between Public and Private: On social media, personal lives often blend with professional identities. A lawyer or psychologist who shares personal opinions in offensive language, even on a personal account, could still be considered to be harming the dignity of their profession.
3. The Temptation of Personal Branding Building a digital image is legitimate, but when professionals are more preoccupied with pursuing popularity than accuracy or responsibility, professional ethics are in danger of being replaced by algorithms.

Mental Health in the Digital Spotlight

Beyond ethical concerns, another increasingly apparent challenge lies ahead: professional mental health. The pressure to always perform, always be relevant, and always receive digital validation creates its own psychological burden.

The phenomena of digital fatigue and burnout arise when someone is unable to detach themselves from public expectations. Professionals can feel anxious if their posts don't get attention, or feel like a failure if they don't post as frequently as more popular colleagues.

This is where self-awareness is crucial. Ethics apply not only to interactions with others but also to relationships with oneself. Maintaining mental health is part of professional responsibility, as a stressed doctor, lawyer, or consultant will not be able to provide optimal service.

Bringing Ethics and Mental Health Together

Classical ethics teaches balance, honesty, and integrity. In a digital context, these principles can also serve as guidelines for maintaining mental health:

- Maintaining confidentiality means protecting trust while reducing the pressure of negative attention.
- Upholding integrity means not getting caught up in emotionally draining imagery.
- Prioritizing the public interest means directing energy to provide benefits, not just seeking attention.

In other words, ethics and mental health are intertwined. Ethics maintain direction, while mental health maintains resilience. Without ethics, professionals can be swept away by the current of algorithms. Without mental health, professionals can collapse, even with the best of intentions.

CHAPTER 7

Ethics in the Digital Space

Ethics in the digital space isn't just a classic theory imposed on a new world. It's the foundation that ensures professionals maintain dignity, even when everyone can judge with thumbs up and comments.

However, ethics alone is not enough. Mental health awareness needs to be an integral part of modern professional ethics. By upholding ethical principles while maintaining mental well-being, professionals not only survive in the digital age but also set an example: true honor comes not from popularity, but from consistent values and a balanced life.

Why Ethics Are Increasingly Important in the Digital Age

The digital space magnifies everything. A single post can reach thousands, even millions, of people in a matter of hours. On the one hand, this presents a tremendous opportunity for professionals to spread knowledge and build public trust. But on the other hand, even small mistakes can be exposed and quickly escalate.

That's why ethics is even more important in the digital age. The principles passed down from Hippocrates to modern codes of ethics are not just rigid rules, but rather guides to keep professionals on track.

In the digital space, ethics is not only a shield, but also a compass. It protects professionals from the trap of image-making, while guiding the use of technology for good.

The Relationship Between Ethics and Reputation

In cyberspace, reputations are incredibly fragile. They take years to build, but they can be destroyed in an instant by a single unethical post. For example, a doctor accidentally posting patient data, or a lawyer posting a careless comment.

Strong ethics will maintain a solid reputation, even amidst the turmoil of public opinion. By adhering to principles, a professional is not easily swayed by the pressures of virality, because they know what is right and what is wrong.

Mental Health as Part of Ethics

When professionals neglect their mental health, they are also neglecting their ethics. A doctor who is exhausted and burned out will struggle to provide the best possible care. A lawyer stressed by constantly comparing themselves to viral colleagues can lose clarity of thought.

Thus, maintaining mental health is an ethical obligation, not just a personal matter. Ethics extends beyond how we treat others, but also to how we treat ourselves. Mentally healthy professionals are better able to maintain confidentiality, are more patient with criticism, and maintain consistent integrity.

Finding Balance in the Digital Space

To survive, professionals need to find a balance between digital engagement and inner peace. This can be done by:

- Realizing that social media is a tool, not a measure of dignity.
- Limit digital engagement to capacity, so as not to erode psychic energy.
- Putting ethics as a filter before every digital interaction.

With this balance, digital space is no longer a threat, but rather a space that can be utilized without destroying one's identity.

Classical ethics remain relevant, even more necessary in this fast-paced and stressful digital age. The principles of integrity, confidentiality, and public responsibility must now be combined with a new awareness: maintaining mental health so that we can continue to serve with a clear heart.

Professionals who combine the two will discover a dual strength: a solid public reputation and inner resilience. Thus, the digital space will no longer be a grueling battlefield, but a platform for conveying the profession's noble values to the world.

Psychological Dimensions in Digital Ethics

Ethics is not just a set of externally imposed rules; it is also rooted in human psychology. Self-determination theory posits that humans have three basic psychological needs: autonomy, competence, and relatedness. These three are also relevant to explaining how professionals behave in the digital space.

1. **Autonomy**
   Professionals want to feel free to choose what they share. However, this freedom must be balanced with ethical responsibility. Not everything is appropriate to share in the digital space, even if we feel entitled to it.
2. **Competence**
   Professionals want to demonstrate their expertise. Social media makes this easier, but ethics dictate that competence be demonstrated within an educational framework, not to belittle others or simply seek recognition.
3. **Connectedness**
   Professionals want to be close to the public. However, in social psychology, excessive, limitless connection can be mentally exhausting. Ethics serve as a safeguard to maintain healthy relationships, preventing them from entering the private sphere or disrupting the balance of life.

Ethics as a Protector of Mental Health

Often, people think ethics only benefits the public. However, ethics also protects professionals themselves. For example, rules about maintaining patient or client confidentiality not only protect them but also prevent professionals from being exposed to public pressure due to information leaks.

The same is true of integrity. A professional who consistently maintains digital integrity doesn't need to waste energy covering up mistakes or constructing a false image. Ethical consistency creates inner peace, as there's no contradiction between the real world and the virtual world.

Ethics, Algorithms, and Identity

In the digital age, algorithms tend to favor content that triggers emotion, sensation, or controversy. This is where ethics plays a crucial role. It serves as a bulwark against professionals falling prey to algorithmic manipulation.

If professionals follow the flow of algorithms without ethics, their identity will be blurred. They may be popular, but they will lose their way. Conversely, if ethics are the foundation, algorithms can still be utilized without compromising dignity. Professional identity will remain intact even under public scrutiny.

Digital Ethics as a New Competency

In recent literature on digital professionalism, the ability to maintain ethics in the digital space is considered a new competency required by every profession. This includes understanding the consequences of posting, privacy awareness, and ethical communication skills on online platforms.

In other words, today's professionals are required not only to be proficient in their fields but also to be digitally literate with a strong ethical foundation. Those who fail to grasp this risk losing their reputation, even if they possess high technical competence.

The digital space is a new and challenging landscape, but the same ethical principles remain. Integrity, confidentiality, responsibility, and respect for human dignity must still be upheld, but the way they are implemented is different.

Furthermore, ethics not only safeguards the public but also safeguards the mental health of professionals. With ethics, we don't have to maintain a tiring double facade. With ethics, we can be present in the digital space without losing our inner balance.

Online ethics aren't just rules, but rather an art of living that combines classical discipline with digital intelligence. Only then can professionals shine under the spotlight of algorithms without losing their identity.

Real Cases in Digital Ethics

1. **Doctor Case and Patient Photos**A doctor abroad once posted a photo of a patient undergoing a medical procedure, even though the patient's face was covered. The photo went viral but also drew criticism. The patient felt her privacy was violated, and the doctor was disciplined. This case highlights that educational intentions cannot be used as an excuse for breaching confidentiality.
2. **Lawyers and Comments on Social Media**In one country, a lawyer made sarcastic comments about the opposing party in an ongoing case. His comments garnered widespread attention, even praise from his followers, but he was ultimately reprimanded by his professional association for undermining the dignity of the law and violating the principle of objectivity. Digital popularity has actually led to a decline in professional credibility.
3. **Psychologist with Sensational Content**A psychologist attempted to gain followers by creating a "quick diagnosis" content for a viral celebrity. While it attracted a large audience, his actions were deemed unethical due to the violation of confidentiality and scientific accuracy. He subsequently lost the trust of his colleagues. This case demonstrates that professional ethics should not be compromised for the sake of public attention.
4. **Positive Case: Educative Doctor**In Indonesia, a doctor consistently creates short health content without touching on patients' personal issues. He discusses general topics in simple language, ethically, and without sensationalism. As a result, he has become a public reference, frequently invited to appear in

the media, and even trusted to contribute to health programs. This case demonstrates that ethics can actually strengthen digital influence in a healthy way.

Lessons from These Cases

First, classical ethics remain relevant in the digital world, particularly regarding confidentiality, objectivity, and respect for human dignity. Second, a reputation built on ethical violations may generate temporary popularity, but inevitably results in long-term harm. Third, professionals who consistently adhere to ethics not only avoid trouble but are actually more respected, trusted, and influential in the long run.

Final Reflection

The cases above remind us that the digital space is not just an algorithmic playground, but also a moral space. Every post is an ethical decision, every comment a reflection of values, and every moment of popularity carries consequences.

By learning from real-life experiences, professionals can be more vigilant and more steadfast in upholding their principles. Because ultimately, ethics is not just theory, but a real safeguard in this transparent and pitfall-filled world.

CHAPTER 8

Privacy

Maintaining Patient, Client, and Public Confidentiality in Open Spaces

One of the fundamental pillars of any profession is trust. A patient entrusts their health to a doctor, a client confides their secrets to a lawyer or counselor, and the public entrusts information to a journalist or academic. Without this trust, professional relationships will collapse.

However, in the age of social media, maintaining trust has become an increasingly complex challenge. The digital space has no closed walls. Every word, photo, or video shared has the potential to be taken out of context and reach a wide audience. What was originally intended as educational material can turn into a privacy violation. What seems trivial can escalate into a reputational crisis.

The Nature of Privacy in the Profession

Privacy isn't just the right to hide something, but the right to control information about oneself. When someone discloses themselves to a professional, they grant limited authority over that information, with the assurance that it will be safeguarded.

Throughout professional history, the Hippocratic oath has emphasized the importance of maintaining patient confidentiality. Modern codes of ethics for various professions extend this principle: not disclosing personal information without permission, even after the professional relationship has ended. The same principle applies to lawyers, consultants, psychologists, and other professionals.

New Challenges in the Digital Era

1. **Education vs. Exploitation**Many professionals are eager to share case experiences on social media for educational purposes. However, often seemingly anonymous details can

still be identified by certain parties. Here, the fine line between education and exploitation must be carefully maintained.

2. **Privacy in the Visual Age**Photos or videos can contain sensitive information, even without your knowledge. For example, a treatment room background showing another patient, or a document being read in a video recording.
3. **Excessive Transparency**Some professionals share clients' or patients' personal information to demonstrate their "success." However, without explicit permission, this practice violates both ethics and the law.

Healthy Boundaries

Maintaining boundaries doesn't mean closing yourself off completely, but rather understanding where the line should be drawn. Professionals need to:

- Recognizing that confidentiality is a client or patient right, not a professional one.
- Ensure that any information shared for educational purposes has been altered in such a way that it is unrecognizable.
- Clearly distinguish between personal and professional content on social media.
- Always place the interests of clients, patients, or the public above personal interests or image.

Privacy and confidentiality are the foundation of trust. In today's open digital space, this foundation can easily be undermined if not carefully maintained. Careless professionals can lose not only their reputation but also the very essence of their profession.

Clear boundaries are not barriers, but protectors. By maintaining privacy, a professional demonstrates respect for the people they serve. By upholding confidentiality, they uphold the dignity of their profession. And by enforcing boundaries in the digital space, they demonstrate that ethics can remain strong, even in a world that is virtually borderless.

Professionalism vs Sensationalism

In the digital space, the line between professionalism and sensationalism is often blurred. What's meant to be educational can turn into a spectacle. What's intended to be beneficial can become a ploy to garner sympathy and popularity.

ProfessionalismIt is a consistent attitude of upholding the values, integrity, and dignity of the profession, despite the temptation to take shortcuts to the spotlight. It adheres to facts, accuracy, and the public interest. Professionalism rests on ethics: refraining from revealing things that could harm the dignity of others, refraining from abusing trust, and refraining from sacrificing values for the sake of the spotlight.

In contrast, sensationalism is an approach that emphasizes shock, drama, or controversy to gain attention. Sensationalism often disregards accuracy, distorts facts, or exposes personal details that should be protected. In the eyes of algorithms, sensationalism may go viral faster. But in the eyes of professional ethics, sensationalism is a trap that erodes long-term credibility.

Cases That Illustrate the Difference

1. A doctor explaining a medical case with epidemiological data, preventive advice, and plain language: that's professionalism. Another doctor posting footage of a patient in an emergency without permission: that's sensationalism.
2. A lawyer who discusses the legal aspects of a public case while maintaining neutrality: this is professionalism. A lawyer who exposes the personal shame of the opposing party for the sake of popularity: this is sensationalism.
3. A psychologist who creates mental health educational content based on theory and practice: that's professionalism. A

psychologist who speculates about a celebrity's condition in public without a direct examination: that's sensationalism.

Psychological and Ethical Impacts

Professionalism has long-term positive impacts: building trust, strengthening reputations, and providing peace of mind for professionals. Sensationalism may bring momentary attention, but it often ends in regret, public pressure, and even sanctions from professional associations.

Psychologically, professionalism creates consistency between internal values and external actions. This fosters a sense of calm, confidence, and sustainability. Conversely, sensationalism creates an inner contradiction: on the one hand, a desire to be seen as credible, while on the other, a willingness to violate ethics for the sake of popularity. This contradiction will eventually trigger stress, guilt, and even the collapse of professional identity.

Maintaining privacy and confidentiality is not just a matter of compliance, but also a reflection of whether a professional chooses the path of professionalism or sensationalism. The digital space will continue to offer a tantalizing dramatic stage, but only those who stand firm on their principles will be able to stand on that stage for long.

The popularity of sensationalism may bring momentary applause, but professionalism commands lasting respect. And that respect stems not from algorithms, but from relentlessly maintained ethical consistency.

Code of Ethics and Obligation to Maintain Privacy

Every profession has a code of ethics that serves as a basic guideline for behavior. While their formulations vary, they all place confidentiality at its core. Confidentiality is not simply a norm of politeness, but rather a moral and legal contract between professionals and those they serve.

1. **In the Medical Profession**The Hippocratic Oath, more than

two thousand years old, includes the obligation to "keep patient confidentiality." Modern medical codes of ethics reiterate that any patient information, whether medical or personal, may only be disclosed with the patient's consent or for legitimate legal purposes. Violation of this is considered a betrayal of the patient's trust.

2. **In the Legal Profession**Lawyers have the principle of attorney-client privilege, which is an absolute obligation to maintain the confidentiality of information obtained from clients. Without this guarantee of confidentiality, clients will be reluctant to open up to their lawyers, making it impossible to fully defend themselves. Therefore, codes of ethics for advocates in various countries require lawyers to maintain client confidentiality even after the professional relationship ends.
3. **In the Profession of Psychology and Counseling**A psychologist or counselor is often the one who reveals their most vulnerable feelings: trauma, grief, or family secrets. The psychology code of ethics requires complete confidentiality of all information, unless there is a serious threat to the safety of others. Outside of these specific circumstances, confidentiality is a non-negotiable principle.
4. **In Journalism and Academic Profession**Journalists are required to maintain the confidentiality of their sources, while academics are required to respect the privacy rights of their research subjects. Both are required to protect information from being misused.

Why is this obligation absolute?

First, because confidentiality is a prerequisite for trust. Without it, patients won't be honest with their doctors, clients won't be open with their lawyers, and clients won't confide in psychologists.

Second, maintaining privacy is a form of respect for human dignity. Each individual has the right to determine which information can be made public.

Third, confidentiality is a bulwark of professionalism. By adhering to it, a professional asserts that they are more loyal to a code of ethics than to the lure of popularity or the pressures of algorithms.

Challenges in the Social Media Era

As human life becomes increasingly digitally documented, maintaining privacy is no longer simply about refraining from speaking. New challenges arise: medical data that can be leaked through apps, legal information that can be shared via text messages, or patients' personal details that can be seen in photos of office spaces.

Therefore, the code of ethics must be understood in a new context: maintaining confidentiality is not only about not leaking, but also ensuring that every digital action does not have the potential to reveal something that should be kept private.

A professional code of ethics is not a negotiable option, but rather a binding obligation. It serves as both a moral and legal safeguard, protecting both professionals and those they serve.

In the age of algorithms, the obligation to maintain privacy becomes even more demanding, but it is precisely there that the quality of a professional is tested. Those who remain faithful to confidentiality demonstrate that the dignity of the profession is far more valuable than mere momentary attention.

CHAPTER 9

Professional Image and Branding

The Difference Between Building an Image and Simply Seeking a Thrill

In the age of algorithms, every professional is inevitably under public scrutiny. Doctors, lawyers, academics, and counselors are now judged not only by their physical work but also by how they present themselves in the digital space. This is where the need for image building or branding arises. However, it's important to understand that image building is not the same as sensationalism.

Professional Image: The Foundation of Trust

A professional image is a public perception built on consistent values, competence, and integrity. This image is not born from mere imagery, but from a tangible track record. For example, a doctor who regularly provides clear and accurate health education will be perceived by the public as competent and caring.

A professional image endures because it's based on quality and integrity. It's not crippled by changing trends or destroyed by a single negative comment, because its foundation is trust built over time.

Branding: Communication Strategy

Branding in a professional context doesn't mean selling yourself, but rather showcasing your values and competencies in a way that's easily recognized by the public. Branding helps people understand who you are, what you specialize in, and what values you stand for.

A lawyer, for example, might build a brand as a "civil rights advocate" or an "international business law expert." A psychologist might build a brand as a "mental health advocate for adolescents." Strong branding not only makes it easier for the public to recognize you but also strengthens your professional standing amidst the information competition.

Sensation: A Misleading Shortcut

Unlike image and branding, hype is an attempt to gain attention through instant means, often at the expense of ethics and substance. It pursues virality, not credibility. It relies on controversy, not quality.

Sensation may bring a quick boost, but it's fragile. Once the spotlight fades, what's left is doubt and disappointment. In the long run, sensation never sustains a reputation; it actually damages it.

Fundamental Differences

Building an image means investing in trust, while seeking hype means gambling with reputation. Image is the result of consistency; hype is the result of manipulation. Branding is the communication of values; hype is the exploitation of emotions.

Sample case

A doctor who creates educational content on children's health with consistency, simple language, and scientific data will gradually build an image as a trustworthy family doctor. Conversely, another doctor who uploads a patient video without permission might immediately go viral, but he or she could lose their license for violating the code of ethics.

Society now judges professionals not only by what they do in the workplace, but also by how they present themselves digitally. Therefore, the choice is up to each professional: build a healthy image and brand, or fall into the hype game.

Image and branding are marathons that require consistency, while hype is a sprint that quickly exhausts energy. In the glare of algorithms, only an image rooted in ethics and integrity will survive.

Practical Ways to Build a Professional Brand Without Falling for Sensation

1. **Know Your Core Values**Branding isn't about creating a new

mask, but about clearly presenting who you truly are. Identify the core values that underpin your profession: integrity, caring, thoroughness, or the courage to stand up for what's right. These values will form the foundation of a lasting image.

2. **Determine the Field of Specialization**The public needs to know where your expertise lies. Specialization makes branding more focused. For example, a lawyer who specializes in family law will build a different image than a business lawyer. A pediatrician will appear different from a nutrition specialist. With focus, messages are more easily received and remembered.
3. **Consistency in Message and Behavior**Strong branding is born from consistency. Don't change direction just because of trends. If you're known as an adolescent psychologist, your content, communication style, and even interactions in public spaces should reflect that. Consistency builds trust, while inconsistency breeds doubt.
4. **Use Educational, Not Provocative Language**Social media is full of provocative content that provokes emotions. Smart professionals choose educational language, which adds value. This distinction is small but crucial: do you want to be known as a trusted educator or a momentary provocateur?
5. **Build a Valuable Digital Footprint**Every post is part of a digital footprint. Ask yourself: if I read this post in 10 years, would I still be proud of it? If the answer is no, it's probably better left unpublished. A valuable digital footprint is a long-term reputational investment.
6. **Prioritize Ethics over Algorithms**Social media algorithms can change at any time, but ethics never change. When deciding whether to share a patient's story, comment on a legal case, or research findings, keep ethics at the forefront of your mind. This way, your branding will not only be relevant but

also respectable.

7. **Focus on Impact, Not the Spotlight**The best professional branding isn't the one that goes viral the most, but the one that makes the most impact. A doctor whose content helps parents understand children's nutrition has built a strong brand, even if it's not always trending. Real impact will always outweigh momentary attention.

Reflection

True branding is about how the world remembers you: whether as someone who brings value or simply seeks attention. Hype may sparkle, but branding built on values and ethics will shine long-lasting.

Real-Life Examples of Healthy Professional Branding in the Digital Age

1. **A General Practitioner**He consistently creates simple health education content, such as diet tips, seasonal disease prevention, and debunking common health myths. He never uses real-life patient stories, but instead focuses on general topics relevant to the community's needs. As a result, the public recognizes him as a friendly, trustworthy doctor, a go-to for many families.
2. **A Lawyer**This lawyer builds his image by sharing easy-to-understand, practical legal explanations, such as those on workers' rights, marriage law, or simple business contracts. He avoids provocative commentary on major ongoing cases, preferring to educate in neutral language. The resulting brand is one of a professional, thoughtful lawyer, capable of bridging the law with people's everyday lives.
3. **A Psychologist**On social media, she frequently shares content about mental health, such as how to manage stress, build healthy family communication, and strategies for dealing with anxiety. She never reveals client secrets, but

instead uses her own experiences as inspiration to discuss common issues. The brand she has built is one of caring, reassuring, and trustworthy.

4. **An Independent Journalist**She uses digital platforms to address public issues in a critical yet objective manner. Each piece of content she creates focuses on data, in-depth interviews, and analysis, rather than gossip or provocation. The resulting brand is that of a journalist with integrity, one who prioritizes truth over virality.
5. **An Academic**This academic built his brand by sharing his research findings in language that the public could easily understand. He also frequently wrote short reviews of current issues from a scientific perspective. In this way, he gained recognition not only in academic circles but also among the general public as someone capable of bridging the gap between science and real life.

Lessons from These Cases All of the examples above demonstrate the same pattern: healthy branding isn't born from hype, but from consistent delivery of benefits, respect for ethics, and adherence to professional values. Popularity may come, but not as a goal, but as a natural consequence of genuine contributions.

Ultimately, every professional will always face two paths: building an image rooted in values or chasing a fragile spotlight. The first path requires patience, consistency, and adherence to ethics. The second path offers instant gratification, but it quickly erodes over time and can easily be destroyed by a single mistake.

The digital space is a giant mirror. It not only reveals what's on display, but also who's truly behind the scenes. The public may be fooled by momentary hype, but in the long run, they'll return to those who are truly trustworthy.

Building a professional brand isn't just about how you appear, but rather about living according to your professional values every day. True branding isn't the result of algorithmic editing, but rather the fruit of consistent integrity.

The most important reflection is this: the algorithmic spotlight is always shifting, but public trust can last a lifetime. Therefore, it's wiser to choose to be remembered as a professional with integrity rather than merely as a digital phenomenon that quickly disappears.

Building a professional image and branding isn't a mere superficial attempt at publicity, but rather a commitment to delivering real value. The fundamental difference between image and hype lies in its foundation: image is born of integrity, while hype is born of an instant desire to be seen.

A professional who adheres to ethical values, maintains consistency, and puts the public interest above personal gain will reap long-term trust. Conversely, those who get caught up in quick sensations or fleeting controversies will find themselves losing the foundation of far more valuable trust.

The digital space certainly offers opportunities to shine, but only those who balance knowledge, integrity, and thoughtful communication will survive. True professional branding isn't about going viral today, but about remaining trusted tomorrow.

Thus, building an image is an investment, while seeking sensation is a gamble. The choice is each professional's: whether to be remembered merely as a fleeting flash in the pan of algorithms, or to be respected as a figure solid in dignity and public trust.

CHAPTER 10

Reputation Disruption

Reputation is a professional's most valuable asset. It's built slowly, through years of hard work, dedication, and consistent adherence to ethics. However, in the digital age, reputations can crumble in a matter of seconds. One careless post, one offensive comment, or one photo taken out of context can trigger a firestorm of public opinion.

The Rapid Disruption of Reputation in the Algorithmic Era While reputations were once damaged through word-of-mouth rumors, they can now be disrupted by viral posts. Social media algorithms accelerate the spread of controversial content, favoring the emotional engagement of anger, disappointment, or sensationalism over neutral content. As a result, a small mistake can be magnified, reproduced, and spread indefinitely.

Why Is One Post So Dangerous?First, because digital posts leave a permanent trace. Even after they're deleted, screenshots can still circulate. Second, the public often judges not the overall context, but rather the most provocative snippets. Third, for a professional, the public associates a single action with their entire integrity. Therefore, a single ethical violation is considered a reflection of one's identity, even if one has a good track record.

Real Situation ExamplesA doctor who unknowingly shares a patient's photo, even with the intention of educating others, immediately draws protests for perceived privacy violations. A lawyer who posts emotional comments on social media about a particular case is seen as lacking impartiality and undermining public trust. A psychologist who briefly comments on a public figure's mental state without a direct examination is harshly criticized by his professional community for being unethical.

All these examples show how fragile digital reputation is.

Psychological and Social Impacts For professionals, losing their reputation means losing trust. Without trust, a profession loses its core calling. The psychological pressure of "trial by social media" can trigger severe stress, anxiety, and even depression. On the social side, a damaged reputation is often followed by the loss of patients, clients, or professional opportunities.

Reputation Maintenance Strategy Facing the risk of reputation disruption, there are several strategies that need to be understood:

- Always use ethics as a filter before uploading.
- Think about the long-term impact, not just the immediate response.
- Strictly separate personal and professional life in the digital space.
- When mistakes happen, admit them honestly and take corrective action, not defensively.

Reputation is the currency of trust, and in the age of algorithms, its value can be lost in an instant. A single post may seem trivial, but its impact can shatter the foundations built over years. Therefore, a wise professional will treat every word, every image, and every comment in the digital space with the utmost awareness.

Trust can't be bought, it can only be earned. And in an era of reputation disruption, that means thinking before posting and putting ethics above popularity.

Reputation Disruption from a Psychological Perspective

How can a single post shatter trust built over years? The answer isn't just about algorithms, but also about how the human mind works.

Negative Effects Social psychology shows that humans tend to remember negative experiences more strongly than positive ones. This is called negativity bias. One bad behavior or mistake will linger in the memory longer than ten previous good deeds. Therefore, when a professional makes a single post deemed incorrect, the public will more easily associate it with that person's overall integrity.

Reverse Halo Effect Typically, a positive reputation creates a halo effect, where the public tends to view everything in a positive light due to initial trust. However, in the digital space, a small mistake can reverse this effect. The halo effect turns into a horn effect: a single mistake is seen as evidence that all other aspects of the person are flawed.

Digital Mass Psychology On social media, judgment is no longer individual, but collective. People are influenced by majority opinion, even when that majority is shaped by emotional narratives or snippets of information. This phenomenon is called social proof. When many people criticize a post, others tend to follow suit without further thought. This is what causes reputations to collapse, not just because of the content of the post, but because of the mass media that forms around it.

Cognitive Dissonance For followers or patients who have long trusted them, the mistakes of professional public figures create emotional conflict. They feel betrayed by someone they should have looked up to. To alleviate this psychological discomfort, they tend to choose to break trust. This is why professional reputations are much more vulnerable, as public trust in them is already held to a higher moral standard.

Psychological Pressure on Professionals For professionals themselves, reputational disruption can cause psychological trauma. Shame, guilt, and the social pressure of public comment can trigger sleep disturbances, anxiety, and even depression. Several cases have shown that loss of reputation in the digital space can impact personal identity, as professions are often closely tied to a person's identity.

Psychological Lessons

From a psychological perspective, maintaining a reputation means safeguarding public perception, which is formed through small symbols in the digital space. Therefore, self-awareness is key.

Professionals need to understand that every post is a representation of themselves, seen by thousands of eyes, filtered by psychological biases, and reinforced by collective opinion.

By understanding these mechanisms, professionals can be more cautious, not only ethically but also psychologically. Because behind every "upload" button, there's a reputational risk that could alter the course of a life.

Tips for Maintaining Your Reputation in the Digital Age

If a reputation can be destroyed by a single post, then maintaining it should be a core discipline for every professional. There are several practical principles you can apply without losing your identity:

1. Self-Awareness Before Uploading Asking simple questions before hitting the upload button can act as a safety net: Is this helpful? Is it ethical? Could it be misinterpreted? If in doubt, don't share. In psychology, this step strengthens self-regulation, which is essential for managing impulses.

2. Separate Personal and Professional Identities Having a private space online is a right, but the professional sphere demands higher standards. Establishing clear boundaries between personal and public accounts helps prevent content mixing, which could lead to reputational issues.

3. Prioritize Educational Values Content that focuses on providing value will be more enduring than mere sensationalism. Professionals can build a reputation by sharing knowledge, experience, or insights relevant to their field. This way, public attention comes not from controversy, but from contribution.

4. Manage your emotions wisely Many reputations have been ruined by comments written in anger or frustration. Controlling your emotions before responding to public issues is key. Psychology shows that taking a short pause to calm down can prevent costly impulsive decisions.

5. Be Transparent in Dealing with Mistakes If a mistake is made, admitting it honestly is better than avoiding it. The public values authenticity and the courage to take responsibility. Transparency can help restore some trust, even if a reputation has been shaken.

6. Consistency in Values and Behavior Reputation is built on consistency. When a professional exhibits the same behavioral patterns across all platforms, both online and offline, the public perceives integrity as a hallmark. This consistency creates psychological stability in public perception.

7. Protect Privacy and Confidentiality The confidentiality of patients, clients, or partners should never be divulged. A single breach of privacy can destroy a reputation instantly. Professionals need to develop an awareness that maintaining privacy is not just a legal obligation, but a moral foundation that upholds the dignity of their profession.

8. Build a Positive Digital Footprint Reputation isn't just about avoiding mistakes, but also about cultivating goodness. Filling your digital space with valuable contributions is the most effective way to strengthen your positive footprint. That way, if a small mistake occurs, the public still has reason to look at your broader track record.

Reputation isn't something that's built overnight, but rather the result of years of consistency, values, and ethics. But in the age of algorithms, that entire edifice can crumble in an instant with just one erroneous post. Awareness of the fragility of digital reputation should be a wake-up call for every professional to be more discerning in their online behavior.

Maintaining a reputation means maintaining trust. And trust is at the heart of every profession: doctors are trusted for their commitment to patient health, lawyers for their integrity in upholding the law, psychologists for their sensitivity to safeguarding client confidentiality and well-being, and journalists for their courage to speak the truth. Once trust is lost, a profession loses its soul.

Therefore, professionals need to instill a simple yet powerful principle: every word, image, or comment shared digitally must be in line with the dignity of the profession. Mistakes can happen, but the maturity to manage emotions, the awareness to prioritize ethics, and the courage to take responsibility are the main pillars that maintain a strong reputation.

Ultimately, the digital world is not the enemy. It is a space that can empower or undermine. The decision rests with each professional: whether to use it as a tool for service and education that expands benefits, or to allow it to become a trap that undermines trust.

CHAPTER 11

Legal Profession

Challenges for Advocates, Judges, and Notaries in the Digital Era

The legal profession has long held a noble position due to its role in upholding justice, maintaining legal certainty, and protecting citizens' rights. However, in the digital age, this profession faces a new challenge: public scrutiny is no longer confined to courtrooms or official documents, but has expanded to the mobile screens of millions. Advocates, judges, and notaries now live in two spaces: the real space of law and the virtual space of algorithms.

Advocates: Between Education and Exposure An advocate is required to defend a client's interests with integrity and professionalism. However, social media often tempts advocates to assert themselves, flaunt their cases, and even express strong opinions on ongoing cases. Advocates are, however, bound by a code of ethics that regulates client confidentiality, independence of action, and the obligation to uphold the dignity of the judiciary. A single emotional post could create a conflict of interest or even be considered a violation of the presumption of innocence.

On the other hand, many advocates have successfully utilized digital media to provide practical legal education to the public, such as explaining workers' rights, inheritance laws, or business contracts. In this way, advocates not only build a healthy image but also expand their social role.

Judge: Neutrality in the Shadows of the Public Judges face a greater challenge. Their duty is to maintain neutrality, rendering decisions based on the facts of the trial and applicable law, not public pressure. However, in the digital age, every judicial decision can be immediately met with criticism, even creating narratives on social media that sway public opinion. This pressure has the potential to affect judges' psychology, although ideally, decisions should remain free from interference.

Furthermore, judges' personal lives are also under scrutiny. Personal photos, posts, or comments can be interpreted as political or partisan positions. Judges are required to maintain a distance from all vested interests to maintain the legitimacy of justice. Therefore, judicial ethics in the digital age is not only about rulings, but also about managing personal image to avoid the perception of bias.

Notaries: Guardians of Legality in the Information Age Notaries, whose duty is to ensure legal certainty through authentic documents, also face public scrutiny. What should be a quiet, behind-the-desk job can now be exposed in the event of a document dispute or accusation of malpractice. The challenge is maintaining trust amidst the rise of hoaxes, digital document forgery, and illegal notarial practices exploiting the internet.

A wise notary can use digital media to educate about the importance of document legality, distinguish legitimate practices from fraudulent ones, and explain the role of notaries in public life. In this way, their role will grow in recognition and respect.

Algorithms and the Moral Burden of the Legal Profession These three professions—advocates, judges, and notaries—are all under pressure from algorithms. They are required not only to be legally correct but also to "appear correct" in the eyes of the digital public. Herein lies the greatest moral test: how to maintain professional integrity without succumbing to the logic of popularity.

The legal profession is not just a job, but a calling to uphold the pillars of justice. In the digital age, the spotlight of algorithms makes this profession increasingly vulnerable to misinterpretation, public pressure, and exposure traps. Yet, it is precisely in these circumstances that a code of ethics must serve as a compass that guides every step.

Advocates, judges, and notaries must not simply follow the tide of opinion, as their duty is not to serve popularity, but rather to serve law and justice. With this awareness, they can remain steadfast as pillars of public trust, even as the digital world continues to change.

The Legal Profession in Today's Era: What Should It Be?

The legal profession has moral and social responsibilities that extend far beyond simply carrying out legal procedures. In today's transparent and fast-paced world, advocates, judges, and notaries are required not only to comply with regulations but also to position themselves wisely in the digital space.

Advocates: Be a Bridge of Education, Not Provocation Advocates should utilize digital media to improve public legal literacy. Simple education about citizens' rights, how to access legal aid, or the fundamental differences between criminal and civil law will be far more beneficial than provocative comments on specific cases. In this way, advocates maintain the dignity of their profession while expanding access to justice for the wider community.

Judges: Maintaining the Neutrality and Dignity of the Judiciary Judges in the digital age are required to maintain their distance from public opinion. Neutrality is not only essential but also evident. Judges' presence on social media should be limited to activities that do not create the perception of bias, such as sharing legal literature, promoting procedural transparency, or educating about the importance of the rule of law. Judges who maintain distance from the din of algorithms will be increasingly respected for standing firmly on the principle of justice.

Notaries: Becoming a Bastion of Legality in the Digital Era With the rise of digital documents and the potential for forgery, notaries need to prioritize integrity and accuracy more than ever. In the digital space, notaries can play a role in educating the public about the importance of authentic documents, the risks of using illegal services, and the legal value inherent in official deeds. In this way, notaries remain relevant while maintaining public trust.

Legal Professionalism in the Algorithmic Era The legal profession should not lose its way despite a changing world. In fact, amidst such intense public scrutiny, the legal code of ethics needs to serve as a beacon. Advocates, judges, and notaries who balance transparency with prudence, openness with integrity, and communication within ethical boundaries will be role models of professionalism in the digital age.

The main thing is In the digital age, the legal profession should act as a guardian of values, not a follower of the current. They must bravely distance themselves from false popularity, refuse to succumb to algorithmic pressure, and uphold integrity as their primary foundation. In this way, the legal profession remains a pillar of justice, even as the virtual world continues to shake it with relentless scrutiny.

Contemporary Case Studies of the Legal Profession in the Digital Age

1. **Lawyers Caught in the Social Media Spotlight**A lawyer defended a high-profile case that garnered public attention. He frequently commented on his personal account, even uploading excerpts from court documents to demonstrate the brilliance of his defense. These posts drew heavy criticism for violating confidentiality. As a result, although he technically succeeded in court, his reputation with the public and the legal community suffered.
2. **Judges Whose Private Lives Were Exposed**A judge who ruled on a controversial case came under intense scrutiny on social media. The public discovered old posts of his social activities with prominent figures and interpreted the judge as being unbiased. Although his ruling was legally valid, public opinion already perceived him as biased. This case demonstrates the importance of careful judges in maintaining their personal image, even outside the courtroom.

3. **Notaries and Digital Documents**A notary was allegedly involved in the legalization of business documents that were later proven to be fraudulent. Although he was not directly involved, social media amplified the issue, accusing the notary of frequently abusing his authority. Public pressure forced him to issue an official clarification and face an ethics investigation. This case demonstrates how digital opinion can influence public perception of the notary's role, even before a formal ruling is issued.

Reflections on These Cases All of the examples above demonstrate that algorithms can shift the focus of public judgment from legal facts to social perceptions. Advocates, judges, and notaries must not only be legally correct but also appear ethical and professional in the public eye. In other words, maintaining a reputation in the digital space is just as important as maintaining integrity in the physical space.

CHAPTER 12

Medical Profession

Doctors, Healthcare Professionals, and Ethics in Online Spaces

The medical profession has been built on a solid ethical foundation for thousands of years. The Hippocratic Oath symbolizes that this profession is not just a job, but a calling to safeguard human life and health. However, in the digital age, the role of doctors and healthcare workers is no longer confined to the practice room or hospital, but also extends to cyberspace, under constant public scrutiny.

Ethical Challenges in the Digital Space Social media offers significant opportunities for medical professionals to provide health education. Many doctors now share health tips, explain diseases, and even promote healthy lifestyles. However, the digital space also holds pitfalls. The temptation to be different, go viral, or sensational often leads some medical professionals to deviate from their ethical guidelines.

For example, using patient stories for content without explicit permission, publicly commenting on patients' conditions, or creating entertainment content that undermines the dignity of the profession. All of these actions can undermine the trust that underpins the doctor-patient relationship.

Doctors and the "Celebrity Doctor" Phenomenon The digital age has given rise to the phenomenon of "celebrity doctors": medical professionals who become popular on social media for their engaging, humorous, or viral content. Some leverage this popularity to disseminate useful health information. However, many end up focusing more on follower numbers than on the quality of their content. This phenomenon creates a dilemma: how to balance popularity and professionalism?

Other Health Workers in Public Spaces It's not just doctors; nurses, midwives, and other medical personnel also face public scrutiny.

Many share their stories online as a form of self-expression, but forget that patient confidentiality is an absolute principle. A nurse, for example, could face sanctions simply for posting a patient's photo (even if the face is blurred) or sharing a medical experience that is deemed a violation of privacy.

Psychological Dimension: Pressure and Temptation From a psychological perspective, digital scrutiny creates cognitive dissonance for medical professionals: on the one hand, they want to appear like ordinary people who can socialize, joke, and gain recognition; on the other, they are bound by a professional oath that demands extreme caution. This tension can become a source of stress if not managed properly.

Medical Ethics in Cyberspace The medical code of ethics clearly states the obligation of doctors and healthcare professionals to maintain patient confidentiality, prioritize safety, and reject all forms of professional abuse. In the digital age, these principles remain unchanged, but are even more crucial. The online space demands that doctors be careful in their choice of words, images, and even humor. Small mistakes can be considered serious violations, and public trust is difficult to restore.

The medical profession is a profession of trust. The public entrusts their lives and health to doctors and healthcare workers, and that trust must be maintained everywhere, including in the digital space. A doctor may be popular, but the most important thing is to uphold their oath. A nurse may express themselves freely, but the dignity of the profession must always be paramount.

The age of algorithms is not a reason to relax ethics, but rather a call to enforce them more strongly. In this way, the medical profession is not only relevant in the real world, but also remains respectable in the online space.

Case Studies of the Medical Profession in the Digital Spotlight

1. **Doctors Who Upload Patient Photos**A doctor at a hospital shared a photo of a patient being treated, intending to demonstrate the medical team's success. Although the patient's face was obscured, the public considered the action a violation of privacy, as medical information should not be shared without written permission. This case resulted in a stern reprimand from the institution where he worked.
2. **Nurses Who Create Entertainment Content in the Treatment Room**A nurse created a short video trending on social media, set in a treatment room. Although it didn't feature any patients, many people considered her actions inappropriate, believing they didn't take the situation seriously. The video went viral, ultimately impacting the hospital's reputation.
3. **Medical Professionals Who Comment Openly About Public Patients**A healthcare professional posted a comment on social media about the condition of a public figure who was ill. Although the intention was simply to provide clarification, the comment was deemed a violation of the code of ethics because it touched on the individual's medical condition without their express permission.
4. **Popular Doctors Who Were Derailed by Sensational Content**A doctor who initially gained popularity for his health education began creating entertaining content to maintain his followers' engagement. He once used a derogatory term to describe a disease, sparking a massive outcry from patients and his professional organization. The popularity he had built over the years was immediately tarnished.

Reflections on These Cases These examples demonstrate a common pattern: initial intentions may be good, but if not based on caution and adherence to a code of ethics, public scrutiny can backfire. In the medical profession, every action in the digital space is not just about content, but also about maintaining the trust inherent in the profession.

Medical ethics is not simply a written code, but a shield that protects the profession's dignity from the onslaught of algorithms. By learning from these cases, doctors and healthcare professionals can understand that digital reputations are inseparable from the professional oath they have sworn.

The medical profession is more than just clinical skills or knowledge, but rather a moral covenant between healthcare professionals and the public. When someone wears a doctor's coat, a nurse's uniform, or other medical attire, they are not only carrying themselves but also a symbol of public trust.

The digital age, with all its spotlight, should not obscure the fact that the core of the medical profession is service, integrity, and confidentiality. Popularity may come and go, and follower counts may rise and fall, but patient trust can only be earned once, and once broken, it's difficult to restore.

Every post, comment, or action online is a reflection of the medical profession's adherence to its ethical oath. A doctor or nurse isn't measured by how much their content is viewed, but by how well they uphold the dignity of their profession while providing tangible benefits to others.

An important reflection for medical professionals in the algorithmic era is: don't let the digital world dictate values, but use them to affirm them. Ethics are not just rules, but the foundation that keeps the medical profession strong, respected, and meaningful, both in the practice room and online.

Behind every white coat and medical uniform lies a responsibility far greater than simply prescribing medication or performing medical procedures. There's an unspoken promise to uphold human dignity, to be a guardian of life, and to put the patient's needs above personal needs.

The spotlight of algorithms may be tempting with the glow of popularity, but that glow is fleeting. What endures is the tangible impact of a healthcare professional's attitudes and actions. Patients won't remember how many "likes" a doctor has, but they will always remember whether the doctor listened with empathy, kept confidentiality, and cared sincerely.

Every healthcare professional in the digital age needs to ask themselves: do my actions online strengthen public trust, or undermine it? This simple question can serve as an ethical compass that guides us amidst the flood of information and the temptation of sensationalism.

Ultimately, the medical profession is a profession of trust. If that trust is lost, the very essence of the profession is lost. And no algorithm, no matter how powerful, can replace the noble values born of integrity, empathy, and wholeheartedly upheld ethics.

CHAPTER 13

Academics and the World of Education

Lecturers, Teachers, and the Challenge of Maintaining Credibility in the Online Era

Education is one of the main pillars in building a civilization. Lecturers and teachers are not only instructors, but also moral guides, guardians of knowledge, and role models for the growing generation. However, in the digital age, the world of education faces new challenges: the spotlight of social media and the logic of algorithms that do not always align with academic values.

Teachers and Lecturers in the Digital Space Teachers and lecturers are now present not only in classrooms or auditoriums but also on students' mobile screens. They teach through online platforms, upload materials to social media, and even participate in viral public conversations. This situation opens up significant opportunities to expand the reach of education, but also raises ethical challenges.

On the one hand, digital media can be a means to disseminate knowledge more widely, providing access to those who previously had difficulty accessing it. On the other hand, when educators focus more on pursuing popularity than maintaining the depth of their knowledge, academic integrity can be compromised.

Academic Credibility in the Spotlight An academic's credibility is measured not only by degrees and publications, but also by how they maintain scientific integrity. Citing sources without citing references, simplifying scientific issues to the point of misleading the public, or offering opinions mixed with personal interests are dangerous forms of credibility erosion.

Teachers and lecturers are often expected to be "concise" and "entertaining" on social media to attract attention. However, if that conciseness is compromised at the expense of accuracy, education becomes shallow entertainment. Academic credibility should not be jeopardized simply for the sake of going viral.

Psychological Pressure in the Online Era Psychologically, educators face new pressures: they are judged not only by students or institutions, but also by the wider public, who can comment, criticize, and even judge them openly. A single misrepresentation can spread quickly and damage a reputation built over years. This often leads to performance anxiety among lecturers and teachers when speaking in digital spaces.

Between Inspiration and Sensation Many teachers and lecturers try to use social media to inspire students creatively. Some succeed in turning their content into an effective learning tool, but others end up trapped in empty image-building. The difference lies in intention and consistency: is the primary goal to educate, or is it simply to seek public attention?

Maintaining Academic Dignity Being a teacher or lecturer in the digital age means being open to the public, but also requiring greater caution. Every statement, post, or interaction should be viewed not only as a personal expression but also as a representation of the profession. The dignity of education depends on academics' ability to maintain a balance between openness and caution.

Case Studies of Academics and the World of Education in the Digital Era

1. **The Teacher Who Went Viral for His Educational Content**A teacher created a short video explaining a math concept in a simple and engaging way. The video went viral and was watched by millions of people, not just her students. This popularity further strengthened her reputation as an educator because she consistently maintained the quality and credibility of her material. This case demonstrates that social media can be a powerful tool for expanding educational

benefits when used for the right purposes.

2. **Lecturer Stumbles Due to Controversial Statement**A lecturer shared his opinion on a hot political issue on social media. His post sparked widespread debate, and some students felt uncomfortable, believing he was no longer impartial as a teacher. While his opinion was private, his academic reputation was also damaged. This case serves as a reminder that academics must carefully separate professional roles from personal expression.
3. **Teachers Who Upload Student Activities Without Permission**A teacher recorded and uploaded a video of her students joking around in class, aiming to show a warm learning atmosphere. However, the students' parents considered the action a violation of their children's privacy. Instead of receiving appreciation, the teacher faced public criticism and a reprimand from the school.
4. **Lecturers Who Create Concise but Misleading Material**A lecturer attempted to simplify scientific concepts for the lay public on social media to make them easier to understand. Unfortunately, the simplification went too far, leading to public misunderstanding of the subject. While his content was popular, his academic credibility was questioned by his colleagues.

Reflections on These Cases From the examples above, it's clear that the digital space can be a golden opportunity to expand academic influence, but also a minefield that can undermine credibility. The key lies in intention, accuracy, and an awareness of professional responsibility. Academics not only teach knowledge but also set an example of integrity.

By learning from this real-life case, teachers and lecturers can understand that the digital spotlight is not just a stage, but a test of the dignity of education.

CHAPTER 14

Consultants, Accountants, and Other Professions

Ethics Amidst Demands for Digital Transparency

Consulting, accounting, and other fields of expertise often directly impact the trust of clients and the public. They are trusted to provide objective advice, maintain data confidentiality, and uphold integrity in every decision. However, the digital era brings new challenges: increased public demand for transparency, along with the risk of openness that can undermine trust if not managed with strong ethical principles.

The Demand for Transparency in the Digital Age The public is now more critical of institutions and individuals engaged in professional services. Accountants are required to report financial information honestly, consultants are required to provide advice without conflicts of interest, while other professionals, such as auditors, analysts, and corporate legal advisors, are required to be transparent about their work processes.

The digital age has amplified these demands. Data can be disseminated widely in seconds, financial reports can be dissected publicly, and a consultant's comments can instantly go viral. Transparency, once limited to client obligations, has now become a public expectation.

Ethical Dilemmas and the Risks of Sensationalism In the midst of public scrutiny, many professionals are tempted to project an "image of transparency" in the wrong way: uploading data, leaking partial information, or making exaggerated statements online in an attempt to appear competent. Unfortunately, these actions can actually damage long-term trust.

Consultants who speak too frequently in public about client cases could be considered a breach of confidentiality. Accountants who try to gain attention by simplifying financial reports on social media risk misleading the general public. True professionalism is measured by the ability to maintain balance: being open as needed, discreet as needed, always ethically sound.

Psychological Pressure: Between Integrity and Public Expectations From a psychological perspective, these professionals often face role conflict between their roles as experts who maintain confidentiality and their roles as public figures who are expected to be transparent. When society demands "revealing everything," while ethical codes demand secrecy, mental pressure arises that can lead to stress or poor ethical decisions.

Professionalism Amidst Algorithms Professionalism means adhering to core values despite public scrutiny from all directions. A true consultant will provide the best advice for clients, not just popular advice. An accountant with integrity will refuse to manipulate numbers, even if it might please their superiors or attract public attention. Any profession based on expertise should place ethics above algorithms.

Consulting, accounting, and similar professions are professions of trust. They thrive not on media attention, but on their credibility and integrity. Transparency is important, but true transparency doesn't mean revealing everything without limits; it demonstrates honesty, accountability, and consistency in their work.

The digital era may change how the public judges, but it must not alter the foundations of professional ethics. In fact, amidst demands for transparency, professionals are challenged to more firmly uphold their dignity, reject sensationalism, and make ethics their unwavering compass.

Case Studies of Consultants, Accountants, and Other Professions in the Digital Era

1. **Accountants and Viral Financial Reports**An accountant shared a summary of a company's financial statements on

social media for educational purposes. However, the summary proved too simplistic, creating a false perception of the company's condition. The public assumed the company was in trouble, when in fact it was not. As a result, the company's reputation was damaged, and the accountant faced ethical reprimands.

2. **Consultants Who Leak Client Information**A management consultant wrote an article about the business strategy of a company he had previously worked for. Although the company's name was not mentioned, the public could easily guess. The article attracted attention, but a former client felt betrayed and terminated their relationship. This case demonstrates that maintaining confidentiality remains a key principle, even when discussing cases in general.
3. **Auditors Who Became Public Figures**An auditor gained popularity on social media for frequently providing critical commentary on the financial statements of major companies. His popularity grew rapidly, but when he was later asked to audit one of the companies he had previously commented on, allegations of a conflict of interest arose. While he technically broke no laws, his reputation was questioned for being perceived as lacking impartiality.
4. **Analysts Who Predict Wrongly in Public**An economic analyst made a bold prediction on social media about market conditions. His prediction went viral, but it turned out to be way off the mark. Not only did his reputation suffer, but public trust in the analytical profession was also affected. This case serves as a lesson that popularity should not compromise scientific accuracy and responsibility.

Reflections on These Cases All of the examples above point to one common thread: digital exposure can magnify a professional's influence, but it also increases the risk of ethical breaches. Client and public trust is the greatest asset of the consulting, accounting, auditing, and analytical professions. Without trust, professionalism loses its meaning.

The era of digital transparency demands the courage to be honest and the wisdom to know when to remain silent. Integrity, not sensationalism, is key to maintaining professional dignity amidst the rapid flow of information.

Consultants, accountants, auditors, analysts, and similar professionals are crucial pillars in maintaining economic fairness, business transparency, and public trust. However, the spotlight of algorithms can quickly turn these noble roles into sensational platforms if ethics are not a primary guiding principle.

True transparency doesn't mean sharing everything without limits, but rather the ability to demonstrate honesty, objectivity, and accountability, while maintaining client confidentiality and professional integrity. Amidst digital pressures demanding instant disclosure, these professionals must have the courage to say: some things shouldn't be made public, because confidentiality is part of integrity.

The important message here is that trust isn't built by popularity, but by consistently upholding a code of ethics, despite online pressure to do otherwise. Popularity may bring followers, but integrity is what earns long-term respect.

In the age of algorithms, professions based on expertise and trust will only remain relevant if their practitioners adhere to ethics. Without them, these professions will be eroded by opinion, lose their authority, and ultimately lose trust.

CHAPTER 15

Public Communication Ethics

Writing, Speaking, and Appearing on Social Media Responsibly

In the digital age, everyone is essentially a public communicator. Through social media, blogs, podcasts, or online videos, anyone can convey ideas and influence opinion. However, for professionals like lawyers, doctors, lecturers, consultants, and others, every word written or spoken carries greater ethical weight. Not only is personal reputation at stake, but also the dignity of the profession they represent.

Public Communication in the Digital Age Writing and speaking in public spaces is now very different from the past. Once, professional speech was only heard in meeting rooms, courtrooms, or lecture halls. Now, a short comment on social media can be read by millions, reinterpreted, and twisted into a new narrative. Algorithms amplify the impact of every phrase, making it go viral or ruining a reputation in an instant.

Therefore, public communication in this era demands greater responsibility. It's not just about what you want to convey, but also how your audience will interpret and use that information.

Ethical Principles in Writing and Public Speaking There are several basic principles that professionals must pay attention to when communicating in the digital space:

- **Accuracy**: ensure that the information provided is correct, verified, and not misleading.
- **Balance**: avoid exaggerating statements for the sake of popularity.
- **Context**: always be aware that digital audiences are diverse; language that is appropriate for one group may be offensive to another.

- **Integrity**: communication must be free from hidden interests that could damage public trust.

Psychological Pressure and the Temptation of Sensationalism Many professionals feel pressure to impress in the digital space: writing bombastically, speaking provocatively, or making sharp statements to go viral. Psychologically, this is related to the human need for recognition. However, when sensationalism replaces substance, public communication loses its value as a means of education and enlightenment.

Communication that is Constructive, Not Destructive Professionals should use public media to build understanding, inspire, and expand knowledge, not to attack, humiliate, or chase instant applause. A concise, honest piece is more valuable than a lengthy, biased opinion piece filled with empty rhetoric.

Public communication ethics is essentially the art of speaking truthfully and responsibly. Every word written or spoken reflects not only one's thoughts but also one's character. For professionals, communication is not just a medium but also a test of integrity.

In the age of algorithms, where words can be both a weapon and a bridge, every professional needs to ask: will what I write and say strengthen trust, or undermine it? This simple question can serve as a moral compass for maintaining meaningful, educational, and dignified public communication.

Words are traces. Once written or spoken in public, they cannot be taken back. In the digital age, these traces are even eternal: stored, shared, copied, and can reappear years later, beyond the control of the writer or speaker.

For professionals, every word represents not only their individual selves, but also their profession, institution, and the ethical values they uphold. One careless sentence can destroy a reputation built over years.

One misguided statement can erode public trust in the profession as a whole.

Therefore, public communication must be treated not simply as free expression, but as a trust. Words can be medicine or poison, they can build or destroy. A professional's responsibility is to ensure that every communication they make brings value: enlightening, maintaining dignity, and strengthening trust.

The most important moral here is: speak with a clear heart, write with pure intentions, and present yourself with integrity. Popularity may come and go, but responsible words will always leave a legacy of goodness.

Real Cases in Public Communication Ethics

1. **A Doctor on Social Media**A doctor shared a medical opinion about a hotly discussed disease. He intended to educate, but instead used derogatory terms about patients. His content went viral, not because it was informative, but because it was perceived as lacking empathy. The public then questioned his professionalism, even though he was scientifically correct. This case is a reminder that truth without empathy can backfire.
2. **Lecturer and Controversial Tweet**A lecturer active on Twitter posted a short comment about a social issue. The comment was interpreted differently by the public and deemed discriminatory. His academic reputation was immediately at stake, and his institution was even dragged into the debate. This demonstrates how context can be lost in the digital space, and a single sentence can create a firestorm.
3. **The Overly Open Lawyer**A lawyer makes public comments about a case he's handling. The goal is to explain the legal position, but some of the information is confidential and shouldn't be disclosed. Opponents exploit the statement,

while the public considers it a violation of ethics. Ultimately, the client loses full trust.

4. **Teachers and Entertainment Content**A teacher made a TikTok video in class for entertainment, featuring the faces of her students. The video went viral, but parents claimed it violated their children's privacy. The teacher initially intended to create a sense of camaraderie, but instead, it was deemed unprofessional.

Concrete Reflection

These examples teach that:

- Public communication is not just about content, but also how it is delivered and its impact.
- Good intentions are not enough; there must be ethical considerations and a full awareness that the digital audience is much broader than the physical audience.
- Every word of a professional is a reflection of the dignity of his profession.

Public communication ethics does not require a professional to be silent, but to speak wisely. It does not forbid writing, but demands that writing bring benefits. It does not prohibit appearing on social media, but reminds us that every appearance strengthens trust, not undermines it.

CHAPTER 16

Algorithms, Bias, and Fairness

How digital systems can create new discrimination

We often hear that algorithms are neutral because they are built on mathematical logic. However, the reality is that algorithms are never truly free from bias. Algorithms are designed by humans, trained on human data, and used in a social context fraught with vested interests. Therefore, when the data used contains inequities, the results will reproduce or even reinforce those inequities.

Algorithms Are Not Neutral Mirrors Imagine a doctor using an artificial intelligence application to analyze a patient's symptoms. If the application's training data comes primarily from a specific population, its diagnoses may be less accurate for other groups. Or a lawyer dealing with a crime prediction system; if the algorithm's training data is biased toward a particular race, gender, or social class, the system may unfairly label that group as more "risky."

A similar situation occurs in job recruitment. Many companies use algorithms to select candidates. However, if the system is trained with data that records long-standing preferences, such as a majority of previous employees being of a certain gender or graduating from a certain university, the selection results will tend to discriminate against other candidates, even those with similar competencies.

New Discrimination in Digital Form This is a new form of discrimination: no longer directly through human treatment, but through systems that appear objective but actually inherit old biases. The difference is that algorithmic discrimination is harder to detect because it's hidden behind complex computational logic. A person might not know that they were rejected for a job not because they lacked competence, but because the algorithm deemed their data "not to fit" the desired pattern.

Ethical Challenges for Professionals For professionals, the presence of algorithms presents a dilemma. Using them provides efficiency, but without critical awareness, it can reinforce injustice. A doctor should not completely hand over clinical decisions to a machine. A judge should not assess a verdict simply because a system assigns a risk score. A consultant should not validate a financial report simply because the software detects it as "safe."

Human Consciousness and Role Justice cannot be entirely delegated to algorithms. Professionals must remain moral filters. Technology can help, but final decisions must be informed by a consideration of values, empathy, and ethical responsibility. Algorithms may be able to process data faster than humans, but they cannot feel suffering, understand cultural context, or weigh moral consequences.

The digital age presents new challenges: more subtle discrimination, hidden behind code. The key message of this chapter is that professionals must not surrender their common sense and conscience to algorithms. In fact, amidst the rapid flow of technology, the role of humans as guardians of justice is increasingly important. Algorithms can calculate, but true justice can only be upheld by conscience.

Real Case Examples

1. **Algorithm-Based Job Selection**A multinational company used an automated system to screen thousands of job applicants. The system was designed to find the "ideal candidate" based on data from previously successful employees. However, that historical data was dominated by one gender and one specific university background. As a result, applicants of a different gender or those who graduated from other universities were systematically scored lower, even though they had equivalent competencies. This

discrimination occurred unnoticed, until it sparked public outcry.

2. **Risk Prediction in Law**A court used software to predict a defendant's risk of recidivism. The system was trained on crime data from specific areas where authorities monitored more frequently. As a result, people from certain social groups were more frequently assigned high-risk scores, not because of individual behavior, but because of biases in the data. As a result, judges could impose harsher sentences on certain groups than others.
3. **Health Algorithm**A hospital uses an algorithm to predict which patients are most likely to need intensive care. This algorithm uses healthcare cost data as an indicator. As a result, patients from lower income groups are perceived as "healthier" simply because they spend less on medical care, when in reality, they often delay treatment due to financial constraints. The system unwittingly reinforces inequities in healthcare access.

Reflection on This Case

The examples above demonstrate that algorithmic discrimination isn't always driven by malicious intent. Rather, it often stems from a blind faith in the "neutrality" of technology. Yet, past data rife with injustice can infect today's digital systems.

For professionals, critical awareness is key. They need to ask: Is this system fair to all? Does the data used represent real diversity? Should the final decision still be reviewed by humans with conscience and responsibility?

Algorithms are indeed created to assist humans, but they never exist in a vacuum. They are born from collected data, from past patterns, and from decisions made by humans in the past. Therefore, as history becomes filled with bias, algorithms will inherit that bias, only in a more systematic, subtle, and more difficult to counter.

The real danger lies not in the algorithm itself, but in the human attitude of completely surrendering justice to machines. This is where professional responsibility is tested. Doctors must continue to prioritize empathy over software recommendations. Judges must continue to weigh conscience above system-generated risk scores. Lawyers, teachers, consultants, and other professionals must remember that their codes of ethics were born long before technology, and that should be their foundation.

The moral here is clear: technology is merely a tool, not a moral arbiter. If professionals are not critical, algorithms will become new machines of discrimination that undermine justice. But when used ethically, algorithms can be allies that strengthen human values.

Ultimately, true justice can never be programmed. It can only be upheld by a human conscience that is honest, courageous, and committed to integrity.

CHAPTER 17

Crisis, Scandal, and Reputation

Strategies for facing the storm of public attention

In the digital age, reputational crises can emerge suddenly. One erroneous post, one distorted statement, or one internal case leaked to the public can quickly escalate into a major scandal. Social media algorithms accelerate the spread, while public opinion can punish more quickly than legal proceedings.

A professional or institution caught in the public spotlight faces not only criticism but also a loss of trust. A reputation built over years can be destroyed in a matter of hours. This crisis cannot be completely avoided, but it can be managed with the right strategy.

Dynamics of Reputation CrisisA crisis typically develops through several stages. Initially, a minor incident occurs, such as an inappropriate comment or information leak. Then, social media algorithms amplify the issue, making it go viral. After that, the public begins demanding clarification, the media becomes more involved, and pressure mounts. At this stage, a professional response is crucial: whether the crisis will subside or escalate.

Public Psychology in the Age of Scandal From a social psychology perspective, the public tends to respond more quickly to negative events than positive ones. One mistake is more easily remembered than a hundred good ones. This is known as negativity bias. Therefore, when facing a scandal, relying solely on past achievements is not enough. What's more important is how professionals handle the crisis honestly, transparently, and responsibly.

Strategies for Facing a Reputational Crisis Facing the storm of public scrutiny requires a balance between communication and concrete action. Some key principles are:

- **Transparency**: Hiding the facts will only make things worse.

The public values honesty, even if it means admitting mistakes.

- **Response Speed**: Prolonged silence allows for speculation and wild narratives. A quick response demonstrates seriousness in dealing with the problem.
- **Empathy**: crises often involve others feeling aggrieved. Showing empathy and concern is far more effective than simply defending yourself.
- **Concrete Action**: statements without concrete steps will be seen as manipulation. Internal reforms, procedural corrections, or other forms of improvement must be demonstrated.

Examples of Crisis Situations

A doctor who accidentally posts a patient's photo without permission could face a storm of criticism. A lawyer who makes controversial comments on television could be accused of violating the code of ethics. A lecturer who makes discriminatory remarks could spark student protests. In all of these cases, the first step is not to be defensive, but rather to introspectively admit the mistake, apologize if necessary, and make amends.

A reputational crisis is the ultimate test of a professional's integrity. It's not just how they fall in the face of public scrutiny, but how they bounce back. Scandals can be devastating, but they can also be turning points for positive change.

The key message here is: reputation isn't measured by the absence of crises, but by how we handle them. The courage to be honest, the willingness to improve, and the consistency in upholding ethical values will be the foundation for a professional to not only survive the storm but also emerge stronger from it.

CHAPTER 18

Building Digital Integrity

Best practices for staying professional online

In an era where the physical and virtual worlds are no longer separate, professional integrity must encompass both. While codes of ethics once applied only in courtrooms, hospitals, classrooms, or offices, they now also apply to social media timelines, online forums, and virtual discussion rooms. Digital integrity is not just about maintaining image, but also about consistency: are the values upheld in the real world also maintained online?

Why Digital Integrity Matters Integrity is the foundation of trust. Without it, even the most powerful skills lose their value. In the digital space, every post, comment, or interaction can strengthen or undermine that integrity. The public now judges professionals not only by their expertise but also by their digital footprints. These footprints are permanent and can reappear at any time, even years after publication.

Best Practices for Maintaining Digital Integrity There are several principles that can help professionals maintain their integrity in cyberspace:

1. **Consistency of Values**What is believed and practiced in the real world must also be reflected in digital interactions. A doctor shouldn't emphasize the importance of patient privacy in the office, only to then leak medical information on social media.
2. **Think Before You Upload**Simple questions like "Is this helpful? Is this a privacy violation? Is this ethically sound?" should be your filter before hitting send.
3. **Maintain Professionalism in Interactions**Debates on social media often provoke emotions. Professionals must be able to

restrain themselves from getting caught up in arguments that damage dignity.

4. **Measurable Transparency**Providing information or education to the public is a good thing, but it must be done within clear boundaries. For example, a lawyer can share legal insights without commenting on specific cases at hand.
5. **Separate Personal and Professional Space**Not everything personal should be made public. Maintaining these boundaries is important to prevent professional identities from intermingling with personal lives, which could pose reputational risks.

Digital Integrity and Social Responsibility More than simply maintaining a good reputation, digital integrity means making a positive contribution to the public sphere. Every professional has the capacity to be a calming voice amidst the noise, a source of knowledge amidst a flood of misinformation, and a moral role model amidst a culture of sensationalism.

Digital integrity isn't a publicity stunt, but rather a reflection of our true character. The virtual world only magnifies who we truly are. If we uphold ethics in the real world, it will be evident in the digital world as well. Conversely, if integrity is neglected, the digital world will hasten its downfall.

The moral of the story is clear: in the age of algorithms, trust is the most valuable currency. And that trust can only be maintained by conducting one's professional life with the same integrity, both in the real world and in the digital space.

CHAPTER 19

Moral Compass in the Algorithmic Era

How to stay grounded in values even as the world changes

Technology is changing at an unprecedented pace. Algorithms dictate what we see, artificial intelligence provides recommendations that influence decisions, and social media shapes the way we interact. Yet, amidst such rapid change, one thing remains steadfast: moral values.

History shows that technology always brings both promise and risk. The printing press enabled the widespread dissemination of knowledge, but also spread propaganda. Television provided entertainment and education, but it could also manipulate public opinion. Now, algorithms offer efficiency and personalization, but they also create bias, polarization, and psychological distress. In situations like these, a moral compass becomes a guide to keep professionals from losing their way.

What is a Moral Compass in the Digital Age?A moral compass is an ethical awareness that guides decision-making, even when technology offers shortcuts or public trends push in a particular direction. It's not a technical rule, but rather a fundamental principle: honesty, fairness, responsibility, and respect for human dignity.

Why a Moral Compass is Necessary In a world driven by algorithms, professionals risk being tempted to follow popular logic: chasing virality, bowing to ratings, or choosing the most profitable option immediately. However, without a moral compass, the trajectory can be drastically off. A doctor could fall into the trap of prioritizing the most viewed educational content over the most needed. A lawyer could choose to appear provocative in the media for popularity, rather than upholding the dignity of the law.

Moral Compass as a BalanceA moral compass acts like an anchor in a storm. It helps professionals weigh: Is this decision ethically sound, not just algorithmically advantageous? Does this choice protect human dignity, or sacrifice it for the sake of digital spotlight? Does this action strengthen public trust, or undermine it?

Maintaining a Moral Compass in the Algorithmic Era There are several practical steps that professionals can take to maintain their moral compass:

- Updating ethical understanding to keep it relevant to new challenges.
- Seek perspectives from multiple disciplines, including psychology, philosophy, and law, so that decisions are not purely technical.
- Get into the habit of reflecting: is every action in line with the values you believe in?
- Cultivate the courage to say "no" to algorithmic pressure that pushes in the opposite direction.

The era of algorithms may bring radical change, but fundamental human values remain unchanged. Honesty remains honesty, justice remains justice, and integrity remains integrity. A moral compass is not something outdated, but the only guide that keeps humans human amidst the onslaught of machines.

Ultimately, technology may advance without limits, but true professionals remain grounded in values. The world may change, but our moral compass must remain firm, for only then can the dignity of our profession and humanity be preserved.

CHAPTER 20

The Future of Professions in the Digital World

Reflection: where professions are headed under the spotlight of algorithms

Each era brings new challenges to the professional world. In the pre-industrial era, professions were anchored by tradition and hierarchy. In the industrial era, professions faced mechanization and bureaucratization. Now, in the digital age, the main challenge comes from algorithms that organize information, shape opinions, and even influence public trust.

The important question that arises is: where is the profession headed as the world continues to change under the spotlight of algorithms?

Professions and Digital Transformation Professions cannot ignore technological developments. Doctors now face patients who come to them with internet search results. Lawyers must adapt to complex digital evidence. Lecturers must compete with online learning platforms. Consultants and accountants face automation that could replace some of their jobs. All of these are signs that professions must evolve, not simply survive.

Ethics as a Foundation for the Future However, there's one thing that must never be lost: ethics. Algorithms can copy information, but they can't copy wisdom. Machines can calculate risk, but they can't weigh fairness. Technology can provide quick answers, but it can't convey empathy. Therefore, in the future, the professions that will survive will be those that can maintain integrity amidst change.

Professionals as Guardians of Humanity The future of professions isn't just about technical expertise, but about being a guardian of human values. A doctor who continues to view patients as human beings, not just medical data. A lawyer who continues to see clients as individuals in need of justice, not just legal cases. A teacher who continues to cultivate character, not just the transmission of knowledge.

Reflections on Professional Direction The digital world will continue to create pressure: to be faster, more popular, more sensational. But the true direction of a profession should not be determined by algorithms, but by its underlying ethical calling. Professions are born not to seek popularity, but to serve. Not to simply conform to trends, but to uphold truth, justice, and human dignity.

The most important reflection we need to take away is this: the future of professions is not determined by how advanced technology is, but by how firmly professionals uphold values. Algorithms may be the new spotlight that rules the world stage, but a moral compass must remain the guiding light.

Ultimately, the future of digital professions will be bright if professionals dare to put ethics above algorithms, humanity above sophistication, and integrity above popularity. That's where the balance between a changing world and enduring values lies.

At the end of this journey, we come to a realization: algorithms may be able to transform the way we interact, work, and even think. They can accelerate information, expand reach, and amplify influence. However, algorithms can never replace conscience.

True professionals aren't the most popular on the digital screen, but rather those who remain true to their values even when the world is pushing them in the opposite direction. Integrity isn't born from the spotlight of algorithms, but from the courage to choose the right path, even if it's not always easy, even if it doesn't always receive applause.

We live in a time where reputations can be shattered in an instant, but also in a time where every professional has the opportunity to be a light. That light isn't a false sense of popularity, but rather a consistent commitment: to serve with heart, uphold the truth, maintain dignity, and refuse to submit to the misleading logic of algorithms.

So, if there is one message that we should take away from this entire book, it is a simple but timeless message: Technology may become sophisticated, algorithms may become more powerful, but a profession will only remain meaningful if it is based on ethics.

This is the climax of our reflection: professions under the scrutiny of algorithms are not simply about surviving the digital storm, but about upholding humanity above the tide of technology. Ultimately, it is not algorithms that will determine the dignity of professions, but the moral choices of professionals themselves.

The most important thing to remember is this: technology will continue to change, algorithms will continue to evolve, but ethical values and integrity are unwavering foundations. Professions are born from public trust, and trust can only be maintained through moral consistency.

Popularity may come and go, and the algorithm's spotlight may shift at any moment, but the dignity of a profession will only endure if it is upheld above all else. Ultimately, what earns a professional respect isn't the number of followers or virality, but rather loyalty to one's calling: serving humanity with responsibility, justice, and humanity.

That is the essence of everything that under the spotlight of algorithms, ethics must still stand supreme.

Epilogue

Every era presents its own ethical challenges. In the age of the steam engine, humans learned to balance industrialization with humanity. In the era of globalization, humans were challenged to maintain their identity amidst the world's interconnectedness. Now, in the age of algorithms, we face a sharp, fast, and uncompromising digital spotlight.

This book isn't just about how professions survive under the pressures of the virtual world, but also about how we, as individuals who choose professional paths, can maintain our identity. A profession isn't just a job; it's a calling, a responsibility, and a promise to society.

Algorithmic scrutiny can create an illusion of image, destroy a reputation in seconds, and distort the very meaning of a profession toward false popularity. However, this is precisely where a profession faces its true test: whether it remains firmly grounded in ethics or slips into the wave of misleading digital trends.

This final reflection reminds us that the digital world is not an enemy to be avoided, but rather an arena to be approached wisely. Algorithms can be tools that expand access, accelerate work, and support services, if used with a strong moral conscience.

Ultimately, no algorithm can replace conscience. No machine can replicate integrity. No technology can replace human empathy.

Therefore, the future of the profession will be determined not by how bright the algorithm's spotlight shines, but by how steadfastly professionals maintain the light of their own ethics. That is the true legacy that will keep the profession meaningful, respected, and trusted, transcending time and technology.

PROFESSIONALS UNDER THE ALGORITHM SPOTLIGHT

Ethics, Image, and Competition in the Digital Age

Author Biodata

Muhammad Ari Pratomois a writer, practitioner, and thinker who consistently focuses on ethical issues, professions, and the dynamics of the digital world. With a multidisciplinary background, he actively observes the intersection of technology, human behavior, and moral responsibility in the algorithmic era.

Through his works, Muhammad Ari Pratomo strives to provide reflective and practical guidance for professional lawyers, doctors, academics, consultants, and other professions so that they can maintain their dignity, integrity, and code of ethics amidst the intense spotlight of social media.

His presence as a writer aims not only to inspire but also to open a space for critical discussion about the future of professions in the digital world. He believes that popularity without integrity is illusory, and that ethical values must be the primary compass in an era of technological disruption.

His commitment to issues of professional ethics and digital reputation has made him known as a figure capable of connecting classical moral discourse with contemporary challenges. As such, his work remains relevant to readers seeking to survive and thrive without losing fundamental human values.

Bibliography

1. Bauman, Zygmunt. Liquid Modernity. Cambridge: Polity Press, 2000.
2. Castells, Manuel. The Rise of the Network Society. Oxford: Wiley-Blackwell, 2010.
3. Eysenbach, Gunther. "Medicine 2.0: Social Networking, Collaboration, Participation, Apomediation, and Openness." Journal of Medical Internet Research 10, no. 3 (2008): e22.
4. Floridi, Luciano. The Ethics of Information. Oxford: Oxford University Press, 2013.
5. Goffman, Erving. The Presentation of Self in Everyday Life. New York: Anchor Books, 1959.
6. Habermas, Jürgen. The Theory of Communicative Action. Boston: Beacon Press, 1984.
7. Kitchin, Rob. The Data Revolution: Big Data, Open Data, Data Infrastructures and Their Consequences. London: SAGE, 2014.
8. Moor, James H. "What Is Computer Ethics?" Metaphilosophy 16, no. 4 (1985): 266–275.
9. Nasrullah, Rulli. Social Media: Perspectives on Communication, Culture, and Sociotechnology. Bandung: Simbiosa Rekatama Media, 2017.
10. Nissenbaum, Helen. Privacy in Context: Technology, Policy, and the Integrity of Social Life. Stanford: Stanford University Press, 2009.
11. Postman, Neil. Technopoly: The Surrender of Culture to Technology. New York: Vintage, 1993.
12. Rifkin, Jeremy. The Age of Access: The New Culture of Hypercapitalism. New York: Penguin, 2000.
13. Turkle, Sherry. Alone Together: Why We Expect More from Technology and Less from Each Other. New York: Basic

Books, 2011.

14. UNESCO. Ethics of Artificial Intelligence: Guidance for Decision-Makers. Paris: UNESCO Publishing, 2021.
15. Weber, Max. Economy and Society: An Outline of Interpretive Sociology. Berkeley: University of California Press, 1978.

Don't miss out!

Visit the website below and you can sign up to receive emails whenever Muhammad Ari Pratomo publishes a new book. There's no charge and no obligation.

https://books2read.com/r/B-A-YQCSD-SRHWG

Did you love *PROFESSIONALS UNDER THE ALGORITHM SPOTLIGHT Ethics, Image, and Competition in the Digital Age*? Then you should read *IMPRISONED ON THE ISLAND OF JAVA A Thousand Dreams in Papua*[1] by Muhammad Ari Pratomo!

[2]

IMPRISONED ON THE ISLAND OF JAVA A Thousand Dreams in Papua

By: Muhammad Ari Pratomo

In the remote areas of Papua, behind the beauty of the untouched nature, lies the true story of a struggle of a child named Sugeng. Since childhood, he only knew makeshift schooling, with a teacher who came once a month and tattered books. Yet, his dreams never faded: he wanted equal education for all Indonesian children. His dreams led Sugeng to FIGHT, "imprisoned" in the land of Java. There, he faced

1. https://books2read.com/u/3GQaPa

2. https://books2read.com/u/3GQaPa

various challenges, from longing for his hometown to being mocked for his different accent. But, behind all that, Sugeng found something valuable: knowledge.

This book is not just an inspiring story about a child. It is a heartfelt cry about the inequity of education in the borderlands. It is a loud voice about the importance of our role, from teachers to the government, to ensure that every child, no matter where they are, receives the same rights. "Imprisoned in Java, A Thousand Dreams in Papua" is a reminder that education is a right, not a luxury. Sugeng's story will open your eyes, touch your heart, and move your soul to be part of the change.

Read, feel, and let this story be the beginning of a thousand dreams that you will fight for.

Read more at https://muhammadarilaw.com.

Also by Muhammad Ari Pratomo

Pengacara Melawan Sistem
Sang Pengacara Rakyat

Standalone
LEGAL MECHANISMS OF FOREIGN INVESTMENT iN NDONESIA
The Daily Pen of a Lawyer
Foreign Lawyers in Indonesia: Between Global Collaboration and Legal Sovereignty
The Final Judgement
Youth at the End of Time – A Guide to a Broken World
Back to Father's Embrace
How to Respect Bali in Its Entirety Binding Legal, Customary, and Mystical Rules Island of the Gods
JAVANESE JUSTICE AND THE SOUL OF INDONESIA A Lawyer's Guide to Culture, Law, and the Hopes of His Nation
Preparation of Lawyers in Indonesia to Face New Transitional Criminal Code
The People's Lawyer
Trending Before You Die
PRAMBANAN Between Myth and Inscription

SAFE TEACHING Complete Teacher's Guide Avoiding Criminalization
NIK THIS NAME IS THE VICTIM A Legal Thriller Based on a True Story of Data Abuse in Indonesia
INTRODUCTION TO INDONESIAN LAW Foundations and Transformation in the Digital and Globalization Era
Our Case : Data Examination Legal Thriller Romance
Love Justice Escape In Prambanan
Poems of a Father's Longing
IMPRISONED ON THE ISLAND OF JAVA A Thousand Dreams in Papua
PROFESSIONALS UNDER THE ALGORITHM SPOTLIGHT Ethics, Image, and Competition in the Digital Age

Watch for more at https://muhammadarilaw.com.

About the Author

Author ProfileName: Muhammad Ari PratomoOccupation: Lawyer, Writer, SongwriterBorn: Indonesia, June 21, 1982Instagram: @MuhammadAriLawTikTok: @MuhammadAriLawYouTube: @MuhammadAriLawLinkedIn: Muhammad Ari PratomoX (Twitter): @MuhammadAriLaw

Read more at https://muhammadarilaw.com.

About the Publisher

PT MuhammadAriLaw Pustaka Nada

is a book publisher based in Indonesia, founded by Muhammad Ari Pratomo—a lawyer, writer, and songwriter. The publisher is dedicated to works that voice justice, awaken empathy, and weave the power of law, literature, and conscience into a global literary movement.

Read more at https://mpnpublishing.com.

www.ingramcontent.com/pod-product-compliance
Lightning Source LLC
LaVergne TN
LVHW090416210926
848480LV00002B/586
* 9 7 9 8 2 3 2 3 1 7 8 3 6 *